SPA[illegible]:
THE BOOK

Princess Vespa has escaped from her wedding to Prince Valium. And she's taken her robot, Dot Matrix, *and* her Mercedes space coupé with her! But now it seems she's heading straight back into trouble – for the wicked Spaceballs, led by the dreadful Dark Helmet and Captain Saundurz, are after her!

Will Lone Starr, hired by King Roland, be able to save the Princess from a fate worse than death...?

Based on the hilarious Mel Brooks' film!

BROOKSFILMS Presents MEL BROOKS' "SPACEBALLS"

Starring MEL BROOKS · BILL PULLMAN · DAPHNE ZUNIGA · DICK VAN PATTEN

Special Appearances By RICK MORANIS and JOHN CANDY

Costume Designer DONFELD Production Designer TERENCE MARSH Director of Photography NICK McLEAN

Co-Producer EZRA SWERDLOW Written By MEL BROOKS & THOMAS MEEHAN & RONNY GRAHAM

Produced and Directed By MEL BROOKS

SPACEBALLS:
THE BOOK

A novelization by Jovial Bob Stine
Based on the screenplay written by
Mel Brooks & Thomas Meehan & Ronny Graham

Hippo Books
Scholastic Publications Limited
London

Scholastic Publications Ltd.,
10 Earlham Street, London WC2H 9RX, UK

Scholastic Inc.,
730 Broadway, New York, NY 10003, USA

Scholastic Tab Publications Ltd.,
123 Newkirk Road, Richmond Hill,
Ontario L4C 3G5, Canada

Ashton Scholastic Pty. Ltd.,
PO Box 579, Gosford, New South Wales,
Australia

Ashton Scholastic Ltd.,
165 Marua Road, Panmure, Auckland 6,
New Zealand

First published in the USA by Scholastic Inc., 1987
First published in the UK by Scholastic Publications Ltd.,
1987

ISBN 0 590 70841 4

Made and printed by Cox and Wyman, Reading, Berks.

ONCE UPON A TIME WARP . . .
DEEP IN OUTER SPACE,
FAR BEYOND THE KNOWN UNIVERSE,
THERE LIVED A RUTHLESS RACE OF
BEINGS KNOWN AS . . .
SPACEBALLS

Chapter 1

Into the dark stillness of space roared the mighty Spaceball Star Cruiser. The monstrous craft made its way through the star fields, the forward rockets pulling section after section after section after section after section after section after section after section after section after section after section after section after section after section after section. . . . *Whew.* . . .

The Spaceball Star Cruiser was way too long to fit into a book this short! Let's just say that it was the biggest, widest, longest spaceship ever built.

On the tail of the gigantic ship, beneath six colossal jets, on the right side of the lower bumper, above the mud flap over the tailpipe was a one-hundred-yard-wide bumper sticker: WE BRAKE FOR NOBODY.

Inside the command module of the cruiser, *Spaceball One*, the dark-uniformed crew members worked tirelessly to keep the giant on course. Laser gunners hunched over their gunsights. Radar operators hunched over their telescreens. Navigators hunched over their map stations.

Colonel Sandurz stood at the command rail, observing them all. "Stop all this hunching, everyone!" he called into the intercom. "You know how Lord Helmet feels about good posture!"

Hearing the name of their feared leader, the crew immediately stiffened and sat up straight. "Much better, fellas," Sandurz told them. "Now everyone try to look just a little more ruthless."

Sandurz removed his cap and scratched his balding head. He wasn't feeling particularly ruthless today. He frowned and kicked himself hard in the shin.

Ahh. Good. The pain made him feel a little more ruthless. He had to be ruthless. The Spaceballs were a ruthless people. And he was on a ruthless mission. Stealing all the air from another planet was pretty gosh darn ruthless — right?

Of course, the Spaceballs weren't really going to *steal* all the air from Planet Druidia. They were just going to borrow it and breathe it for ten thousand years or so. Still, it was ruthless.

Sandurz pinched himself real hard. He was feeling soft and flabby. It wasn't the way he wanted to feel. He wondered how others could be ruthless all day long and not even get tired. He wondered what exactly *ruthless* meant.

He'd have to look it up someday. But not today. He remembered he'd left the dictionary on the other end of the spaceship. It would take months to walk over and get it.

He was about to kick himself again, when he was interrupted by the voice of the radar operator. "We're coming up on Planet Druidia, sir."

"Excellent," Sandurz replied, stopping himself awkwardly in midkick, nearly falling off the bridge. "Have you notified Lord Helmet?"

"Yes, Colonel Sandurz," broke in the voice of Ricco, the radio operator. "He's on his way."

Suddenly, guards' voices echoed in the narrow passageway outside the control center. "Make way for Dark Helmet! Make way for Dark Helmet!"

Colonel Sandurz nervously positioned his uniform cap back onto his head. The entire crew snapped to attention and looked fearfully toward the command module's black sliding door.

Heavy footsteps. The door whooshed open. In stepped the unusual figure of their powerful leader, Dark Helmet.

Whoever had named Dark Helmet had done a darn good job. The fierce Spaceball leader wore the biggest, darkest helmet in the universe.

Dark Helmet wheezed heavily as he entered the chamber. The faces of the crew filled with terror as he clomped past them, choking and wheezing. The control center echoed with the sound of his wheezing as he strode up to the command rail.

He stopped next to Colonel Sandurz. He wheezed for a while. Then he did some truly hideous gasping.

Finally, Dark Helmet's hand reached up and ripped off his black visor mask. "I can't breathe in this *fershlugginer* thing!" he cried. He did some more gasping and choking.

Sandurz waited for Lord Helmet to catch his breath. Then he told him, "We're approaching Planet Druidia, sir."

Dark Helmet stopped coughing and looked up at Sandurz. Sandurz could see his little head inside the gigantic helmet. He was all sweaty in there.

"That's good news," Dark Helmet said. "I'll call Spaceball City and inform President Skroob immediately."

"I've already called him, sir," the radio operator, Ricco, interrupted. "He knows everything." Ricco flashed Lord Helmet a toothy smile.

Dark Helmet's face darkened. He looked down at Ricco. "You told the President before you told me?"

"Y-yes, sir," Ricco replied. His smile faded quickly. He began to tremble.

Dark Helmet was furious. "Sergeant Ricco — are you telling me that you went over my helmet?"

"Well, uh, not exactly over. More to the side . . ." Ricco replied weakly. "Sorry, Lord

Helmet. It won't happen again. I promise you — "

Dark Helmet quickly took a black onyx ring with a gold "S" on it out of his pocket and placed it on his right middle finger.

Horrified, Ricco backed away. "No, sir. No!" he cried, raising his hands in a desperate plea. "Not *that*!"

Dark Helmet smiled. "Not *that*? Of *course*, that! What *else*?" Then the evil leader raised the ring, aimed it carefully, and sent out a laser blast that dropped Ricco to the floor, screaming his head off and writhing in pain.

"Mother of Mercy, can this be the end of Ricco?" the unfortunate crew member cried.

Sandurz stared at the unfortunate Ricco. "Wow! What a punishment!" he cried.

"Yeah, I know. I let him off easy," Dark Helmet said, shrugging his helmet. "What can I say? He caught me in a good mood."

The evil leader realized that some of the crew were staring at him accusingly as Ricco continued to roll around on the floor, howling in agony. "Hey — don't look at me like that," Lord Helmet called to them. "What do you expect — *My Little Pony*? I'm not a cuteypie. I'm a bad guy — remember?"

"Yes, Lord Helmet, sir," the crew replied in unison.

"Owwwwwwwwch, sir," replied Ricco.

Having demonstrated what a ruthless guy he was, Dark Helmet turned back to the Colonel. "Sandurz," he called, "I don't see Planet Druidia. Where is it?"

"We don't have visual contact yet, sir," Sandurz told him. "But we have it on the radar screen. I'll punch it up for you."

"Never mind. I'll do it myself."

Dark Helmet stepped up to the complicated console and began to push buttons. Lights began to flash. The machine began to beep. A strange bubbling sound could be heard.

"What's the matter with this thing?" Dark Helmet yelled angrily. "What's all that churning and bubbling? You call this a radar screen?"

"No, sir," said Sandurz. "We call it 'Mr. Coffee.' "

Dark Helmet stepped back. He had been operating the coffee machine. "I knew that!" he cried. "I always have coffee when I look at radar! Now . . . where's 'Mr. Radar'?"

Sandurz pointed him toward a different console. A sign above the screen read: MR. RADAR. Dark Helmet began to push buttons. The Planet Druidia appeared on the screen. "Switch to teleview," Dark Helmet commanded.

Planet Druidia came into clear view. Everyone could see that it was a beautiful planet of blue skies and fluffy white clouds inside a huge Plexiglas air shield.

"There it is — Planet Druidia," Dark Helmet said, staring at the screen. "And inside the air shield — ten thousand years of fresh air. We *must* get through that air shield!"

"We will, sir," Sandurz said enthusiastically. "Once we kidnap the Princess, we can force her father, King Roland, to give us the combination to the air shield."

"Everybody hear that important plot point?" Dark Helmet asked.

"Yes, sir," everyone answered in unison.

"Owwwwwwch, sir," answered Ricco.

Dark Helmet turned back to Sandurz. "When is the Princess to be married?"

"Within minutes, sir," Sandurz replied.

"Good." An evil smile crossed Dark Helmet's sweaty little face. "I hope it's a long ceremony — 'cause she's gonna have a short honeymoon!"

He tilted his head back in an evil laugh, and the visor slammed down over his face. Coughing and wheezing, he struggled to open it. "Help me! Gasp! Get me out!"

Thinking quickly, Colonel Sandurz reached into his uniform jacket and pulled out a can opener. A few seconds later, he had pried Lord Helmet's visor open.

As soon as he could catch his breath, Dark Helmet began his evil laugh all over again.

Chapter 2

In the royal bedchamber of Vespa, Princess of Planet Druidia, everything softly glowed and shimmered. Vespa's room was like a fairy tale, and Vespa looked like a fairy tale princess, with soft, flowing brown hair; dark, shimmering eyes; and rosebud red lips. On this day, however, her wedding day, Vespa could think of only one fairy tale — *Beauty and the Beast*.

"I can't marry him, Dot. I don't love him. I don't even like him," the Princess said, her eyes brimming with tears.

Dot Matrix, her faithful droid, continued fussing with the Princess's wedding veil. Dot was all dolled up, bright and sparkling like gold. She had poured an entire can of metal polish in her bath! Dot wanted to shine. She was Droid of Honor, after all.

"Oh, why did I have to be born a princess?" Vespa moaned, throwing herself unhappily down onto a feather footstool. "Why couldn't I have been born a peasant . . . an incredibly wealthy peasant. Then I'd be free . . . to marry the man of my dreams."

"The man of your dreams?" the droid asked, sounding surprised. "You know him? You've seen him?"

The Princess shook her beautiful head sadly. "No, I haven't met him yet. But he's got to be out there . . . somewhere. . . ." Vespa gazed longingly out the window, up toward the sky. "Somewhere. . . ."

At that very moment, about a million miles above the Princess's castle, a battered, dust-covered Winnebago-type flying camper chugged noisily through a galaxy of stars. Amazing as it may seem, the stars formed the word *somewhere*.

The flying Winnebago was not exactly the sleekest spacecraft in the galaxy. On its roof was a rabbit-ears TV antenna. On the side of the camper, someone had written in the dust: PLEASE WASH ME.

On the dented cockpit door were the words: *EAGLE FIVE*. Beneath the words was a large painted insignia — a screaming eagle clutching dollar bills in each claw, above the words: CAPTAIN LONE STARR — HERO FOR HIRE. In the side window was a small, head-lettered sign that read: NO RADIO.

The interior of the *Eagle Five* was no better looking than the exterior. Dirty clothes and empty cans littered the cabin. An inch of dust settled over everything, and a sinkful of greasy dishes was piled nearly to the ceiling.

His boots up on the control panel, his hat pulled down over his face, Captain Lone Starr was catching a bit of shut-eye.

The phone on the panel began to buzz loudly. Lone Starr ignored it at first. But the buzzing persisted. He groaned, pushed his hat back, and tried to open his eyes. He was a young man, handsome beneath a two-day stubble of beard. He groaned again and shook his head. He was not in great shape. In fact, he was a wreck. Why didn't that buzzing stop?

His eyes still only half open, Lone Starr reached under the dashboard into a small refrigerator and pulled out a cold can. He fumbled with it until he managed to flip the top, then took a long swig, and answered the phone.

"You have reached *Eagle Five,*" he said into the receiver, trying to sound like a recording. "Captain Lone Starr is not at home right now. Please leave message when you hear the sound of the burp."

Lone Starr burped loudly and hung up the phone. Then he pulled his hat back down over his bloodshot eyes and tried to get back to sleep.

The flying camper continued to chug along on automatic pilot. But a few seconds later, the phone began buzzing loudly again.

Lone Starr groaned and called, "Barf! Barf!"

The grease-stained curtain behind the cockpit opened, and in stepped Barf. Half human, half golden retriever, the three-hundred-pound Barf wagged his tail enthusiastically. "Yeah, boss," he growled. "Whaddaya want?"

"Barf, answer the phone," Lone Starr said. He groaned from the effort to form words. "Where you been?"

"Grabbing myself a snack," the big hairy creature replied. "Want a Milkbone?" He held up a box of Milkbone biscuits "For Really Large Dogs."

The phone buzzed again. And again. Barf began to scratch himself as he bit into the dog biscuit.

"Hey — have you got fleas again?" Lone Starr asked. He grabbed quickly for a can of flea spray.

"Who, me??" Barf cried, leaping back, his doggie eyes filled with fear, staring at the threatening spray can. "No. No way! I just got a little itch!"

Lone Starr looked away. Barf began to scratch furiously, biting at his fur. Lone Starr turned back. Barf stopped in mid-scratch, flashing Lone Starr a big grin, pretending he hadn't been doing anything.

Lone Starr gave Barf a suspicious look. It wouldn't be the first time the mangy creature had tried to hide his fleas. "Are you gonna answer that phone?" Lone Starr asked irritably.

"Yeah, yeah. I'll put it on picture," Barf said. He pushed a button on the control panel. A large telescreen lit up, revealing the shiny, stainless-steel face of a gangster droid named

Vinnie. Vinnie was smoking an aluminum cigarette.

"Hello, Vinnie," Lone Starr groaned, not at all pleased to hear from this caller. "What do you want?"

"It's not what I want. It's what *he* wants," Vinnie said.

"Who wants?" asked Barf, looking confused.

As Lone Starr and Barf stared at the screen, an evil-looking fat-faced creature pushed Vinnie roughly aside and moved up close. The pudgy creature was half pizza, half man.

Lone Starr recognized him immediately. "Uh-oh! It's Pizza the Hutt!"

Pizza the Hutt munched on a slice of pizza for a while. Then his fat lips formed a cheesy sneer. "Well, well. If it isn't Lone Starr and his sidekick, Puke."

"That's Barf," Barf corrected him.

"Barf, Puke — whatever. . . ." Pizza the Hutt sneered.

"Pizza, what a nice surprise," Lone Starr said, his voice rising two or three octaves. He looked frightened — because he *was* frightened. "Hey, don't worry. We're workin' like crazy. You'll have your hundred thousand space bucks by next month . . . uh . . . next week . . . next day . . . tomorrow. Definitely tomorrow."

"Cross his heart, he hopes to die," Barf added, trying to sound really sincere.

"A hundred thousand? Unh-uh, pal. You

got it wrong." Pizza the Hutt's face slid into a crooked smile. "When you borrow from the Hutt, you got to add a certain amount of interest, compounded hourly — plus late charges. Hmmm . . . that comes to. . . . Let me see. . . ."

Pizza wet his forefinger and began to punch Vinnie in the eyes with it. A clicking sound came from Vinnie's head as Pizza entered numbers on him, and a stream of white printout paper began to roll out of his mouth.

Pizza ripped off the printout paper and read it to Lone Starr. "You owe me exactly . . . one million spacebucks."

"A *million*?" Lone Starr cried. "That's unfair."

"I wouldn't call it unfair," Pizza said. "I'd call it outrageous!" He giggled. Cheese jiggled and tomato sauce splashed as he laughed. "But you're gonna pay up — or else."

"Or else?" Barf asked timidly.

Pizza the Hutt grinned. "Or else. . . . Tell 'em, Vinnie."

Vinnie stepped forward. "Or else, Pizza's gonna send out for *you*!"

Pizza's grinning face faded away. The screen went black. But Lone Starr and Barf stared at it without moving for a long, long time.

Chapter 3

All of the bells on Planet Druidia chimed out in celebration as Princess Vespa's wedding day dawned. As the warm yellow sun slowly rose in a clear sky, birds added their musical trills to the symphony of chimes. A gentle wind greeted the invited wedding guests, the air sweet and fragrant.

Outside the First Intergalactic Temple (Reformed) of the Druids, the sign read: TODAY — THE ROYAL WEDDING OF PRINCESS VESPA TO PRINCE VALIUM. TOMORROW — BINGO.

Royal footmen were busily heaving case after case of the Princess's matched luggage into the trunk of the royal *Honeymoon Coupe*. The *Coupe* was a simple two-passenger spaceship with a Mercedes emblem on the hood. The license plate read: SPOIL'D ROTT'N 1.

Inside the majestic church the wedding guests buzzed with excitement, waiting for the ceremony to begin. Prince Valium, with his blond pageboy haircut, stood at the altar, awaiting his bride, wondering what all that strange buzzing was.

The organist began to play "The Wedding March." The guests looked to the aisle to see the bridal party enter.

The Princess, bedecked in a magnificent wedding gown of flowing white lace, stepped up to the aisle at the rear of the church. She was being pushed by the King, with help from a fussy head usher.

"Push a little harder," the King commanded. "The music has already started." He looked around. "What's all that buzzing? It's giving me a royal headache."

"No, wait," said Princess Vespa nervously, gripping her father's arm. She peered through her wedding veil. "Where's my Droid of Honor?"

"Oh, dear, yes! Where's Dot Matrix?" the usher cried. He began running frantically from side to side, calling, "Dot! Dot Matrix!"

A few seconds later, Dot came running toward them. "Sorry. I had to make a pit stop," she said. "I'm so excited, I can't hold my oil!"

Dot fell into place behind the Princess and picked up the beautiful lacy train of the wedding gown. "All right, people. It's magic time," gushed the head usher. "Starting on the left foot — go."

King Roland stepped off on his right foot.

"Wrong foot. Wrong foot," said the Princess. "I guess we'll have to call the wedding off!"

"Keep walking," the King commanded.

They took exactly four steps and then stopped. The organist stopped playing. The confused guests turned to see what the problem was.

"Daddy, *must* I go through with this?" Vespa asked.

King Roland gave her a stern look. "I'm sorry, my dear, but you have to."

The organist started up "The Wedding March" again. The Princess and her party began to walk down the aisle again. Four steps later, the Princess stopped. "But, Daddy, I don't love him," Vespa protested.

The King sighed. "I'm sorry, Vespa. But he's the last prince left in the galaxy."

At the front of the church, Prince Valium turned to greet his bride. With sleepy, half-closed eyes, he began to give her a big smile. But halfway there, the smile became a loud, openmouthed yawn.

It was now obvious to just about everyone why Valium was the last prince in the galaxy to get married!

Beneath her veil, Vespa's face revealed her unhappiness. But as she continued her walk down the aisle, she realized she had no choice.

The music stopped. The King stepped aside. Vespa continued walking slowly to the altar with Dot right behind, carefully holding her train.

"Dearly beloved," began the minister before Vespa had even come to a stop. "We are gathered here together on this joyous occasion to witness. . . .”

Vespa reached the altar — and kept walking. She walked past Prince Valium. She walked past the minister. Then she began to run. She ran as fast as she could, pulling Dot behind her.

“We are gathered here to witness... Princess Vespa going right past the altar, *running* out the back door, leaving all of us dumbfounded — especially poor Prince Valium standing here grinning like an idiot. Amen,” said the startled minister.

“Amen,” said the wedding guests.

“Stop! Stop her! Someone stop her!” King Roland screamed, his face a royal purple with rage.

Princess Vespa, with Dot still holding the train to her wedding gown, ran across the parking lot and up the ramp to the waiting *Honeymoon Coupe*. “Wait a minute! Didn’t we forget somebody?” Dot cried.

But Vespa wasn’t about to wait for anyone! She pulled Dot into the spaceship. The ramp pulled up and closed like the door to an airplane.

“Stop! Come back!” wedding guests shouted from below. But their pleas were drowned out by the roar of the engines. They watched in disbelief as the craft tilted up on its launching pad.

King Roland, followed by Prince Valium, ran toward the launching pad. But they were too late to stop the Princess’s escape.

"Vespa, I love you! Come baaa — " Prince Valium started, but his words ended in another long, openmouthed yawn.

With a deafening roar, twin bursts of flame carried the *Honeymoon Coupe* up into the sky. Soon it was only a dark speck between the white clouds.

Prince Valium finished his yawn. "This never happened to me before," he said, his eyes sleepily following the spaceship as it disappeared into the skies. "I'm not sure I know what to feel."

"How about 'humiliated'?" suggested the King.

"Yeah. Humiliated," the Prince agreed, yawning. "That's good. Humiliated. Very good. I guess that's why you're the King, huh?"

Chapter 4

Spaceball City, the capital of Planet Spaceball, looked like a Ping-Pong game that got out of control. The buildings were all white globes that seemed to bounce off in different directions from the rocky terrain.

Inside the largest Ping-Pong ball was the office of President Skroob, leader of the Spaceballs. Short and rather comical-looking, with a raspy voice and a crooked little mustache, Skroob seemed more like a TV or movie comedian than a national leader.

But Skroob was not feeling too comical today as he spoke into the phone to a TV reporter. "Don't be ridiculous," he yelled into the phone. "You can assure your viewers that there is absolutely no air shortage whatsoever. Good-bye."

Skroob slammed down the receiver. Then, making sure no one was watching him, he unlocked a lower desk drawer and pulled out a light green can. The label on the can revealed it to be "Perri-Air." Smiling in eager anticipation, Skroob popped the top, raised the can to his nose, and breathed deeply.

His smile became a satisfied grin. Nothing like air, if you want to do a little breathing, he thought. And this imported stuff was so light, so low-calorie.

Suddenly, the interoffice telewall lit up, interrupting his breathing. Skroob quickly tossed the can behind him.

A beautiful young woman in a military uniform appeared on the screen. "President Skroob, this is Central Control," she said. "Spaceball Commanderette Zircon speaking, sir."

Skroob's eyes bugged out of his head, and his mustache began to twitch. "This Zircon is a gem!" he told himself. He always was a fool for a uniform — especially if the uniform had a woman in it!

"What is it?" Skroob asked, drooling at the wall screen.

"We have just received word from the Spaceball Star Cruiser, sir," Zircon told him. "Lord Helmet informs us that Princess Vespa's *Honeymoon Coupe* has blasted off from Druidia. The ship is in sight, and *Spaceball One* is closing in on her."

I'd like to close in on *you*, Skroob thought, staring at Zircon on the screen.

"You can watch both ships on the teledar, sir, if you wish to observe," Zircon said.

"Yes, I wish to observe. I love to observe. That's my hobby, you know — observing,"

Skroob said enthusiastically. "I'll be right there."

"Shall I have Snotty beam you down, sir?" Zircon asked.

Skroob hesitated. What was this beaming down stuff? And who was Snotty and how did *he* get into this story?

"I don't know about this beaming down stuff," he told her. "Is it safe?"

"It's as easy as breathing, sir," Zircon told him.

Uh-oh, Skroob thought. "Oh, well. Okay. I'll try it."

Skroob stood up and walked over to a small circular platform next to his desk. He opened a sliding door and entered a Plexiglas cylinder.

"Okay, Snotty — beam him down," Zircon commanded.

"Yessir. Immediately, sir," replied Snotty.

Skroob looked up to the top of the narrow cylinder, a worried expression on his face. Suddenly, a ray of green light shot down from the top of the cylinder. The light surrounded Skroob.

"Ooh, that feels good. That feels GOOD! I like it so far!" the Spaceball President declared.

The green light grew brighter, denser. Skroob began to disappear. The top of his head vanished. His chin, his neck, his shoulders — all of him faded away. In seconds, the cylinder appeared empty.

In the Spaceball Control Center, Snotty and Zircon stood beside another cylinder, identical to the one in Skroob's office. As they anxiously watched, the cylinder began to hum. A green ray of light filled the cylinder. Skroob began to appear — first the feet, then the legs, then the waist — until all of him stood before them.

"Good lord! What happened to his head?" Snotty cried.

"I don't believe this!" Zircon exclaimed. "It's on backward!"

"Do something!" Skroob cried from inside the cylinder. His body faced front. His head faced the back. "This is terrible! Why didn't anybody ever tell me my behind was so big!"

"Hold still, sir," Snotty called. "We're going to reverse the beam."

Snotty pushed a lever, and a few seconds later, Skroob appeared — face forward — back in the cylinder in his office. He tried his head out, moving it left, then right, up, and down. It seemed to work pretty well.

"Shall we beam you again, sir?" Zircon's image on the wall asked.

"Forget it," Skroob said, still testing his head. "This time, I'll walk."

He walked over to the door to his office, opened it, and stepped into Spaceball Control Center. It was right next door the whole time!

"Now, where's Princess Vespa?" Skroob asked, walking up to the teledar screen.

"Right there, sir," Zircon told him, pointing to a green dot on the screen.

"She looks a little green. Maybe the wedding cake made her a little nauseous," Skroob said.

"No, sir. That's not the Princess. That's her spaceship," Zircon said patiently.

"What's that other green dot?" Skroob asked, walking up closer to the screen.

"That's our cruiser, *Spaceball One*, sir. As you can see, the Princess is approaching *Spaceball One* at fifteen hundred light leagues per minute."

"Good, good," Skroob said, studying the screen. "Well, that's perfectly clear. I have just one other question."

"What's that, sir?" Zircon asked.

"What the heck is a light league?"

Chapter 5

Princess Vespa, still in her wedding dress, feverishly worked the controls of her small spaceship. Little did she realize, as she guided the ship through the darkness of space, that she was being watched — watched and followed. The evil Spaceballs in their gigantic cruiser were closing in, preparing to kidnap her.

The Princess tore off her wedding veil, revealing a familiar hairstyle. Two large braided buns covered her ears. She looked a little like a princess from long ago in a galaxy far, far away.

"Do you realize what you've done?" Dot Matrix screamed at her. Dot was still in a state of mechanical shock. "Are you listening to me?" Dot cried. "Turn that thing off!"

Vespa removed the two huge buns from her ears. They weren't hair — they were headphones to her royal Walkman. Loud music poured out of them. "What do you want?" Vespa asked, eyes on the controls.

"Who made that man a gunner?" Dark Helmet asked angrily.

A cross-eyed Major turned to Dark Helmet. "I did, sir. He's my cousin," the Major said, staring intently at his own nose.

"And who are you?" Dark Helmet asked, taking a step back.

"He's an Idiot, sir," Sandurz said.

"You bet he is," Dark Helmet agreed.

"No, sir," protested Sandurz. "That's his name. Major Idiot."

"And his cousin?" Dark Helmet asked.

"He's an Idiot, too," Sandurz said. "Gunner's-Mate First Class Idiot. His uncle is on board, too, sir."

"He's also an idiot?" Dark Helmet asked.

"No doubt about it, sir," Sandurz replied enthusiastically. "Sergeant-Major General Idiot."

Dark Helmet threw up his hands inside his helmet. "I knew it," he cried. "I'm surrounded by idiots!"

Chapter 6

As the *Eagle Five* continued to clatter its way across the twisted galaxies of space, Lone Starr and his hairy companion received a surprising telescreen transmission. In fact, when the face of King Roland appeared on the screen, Lone Starr was so startled, he nearly opened both eyes!

"You've got to help me, Lone Starr," King Roland pleaded. "My daughter just called me — collect. You've got to save her. She's being attacked by Spaceballs!"

Lone Starr shook his head. "Spaceballs? Forget it. Too dangerous. I'm already number one on Dark Helmet's hit list as it is."

"Number one with a bullet," Barf said, and then slapped his knees as if he'd made the best joke in the universe. When the half-human, half-dog creature finally stopped laughing, he turned to Lone Starr. "Tell him no. We don't need it."

"Lone Starr, you must!" King Roland pleaded, crown in hand. "You're the only one who can do it. I'll pay anything. Do you hear me? *Anything*!"

"Tell him yes. We need it," Barf said.

Lone Starr looked up at the telescreen. "Anything?" he asked, dollar signs spinning in his bloodshot eyes. "Okay. We'll do it for a million."

King Roland dropped his crown and almost his teeth. "A million?? I said anything — not a million!"

Lone Starr reached up to turn off the transmission.

"Okay. All right. I'll pay it!" the worried King cried. "Only find her. Save her!"

"All right, King. You just made a deal," Lone Starr said, trying to keep his voice steady and calm. Under the control board, he shook hands with Barf. "One princess for one million spacebucks." Just the amount he needed to pay back Pizza the Hutt!

"What's your daughter driving?" Lone Starr asked.

"A brand-new white Mercedes," King Roland told him. "Two thousand-and-one SEL, limited edition, moon roof, a cellular Princess phone. . . . I got a very good deal. I paid cash. My cousin, Prince Murray — "

"We get the idea," Lone Starr interrupted. "Hey — wait a minute. Wait a minute. What was her last position?"

"She was sort of bent over and running as fast as she could," the King replied.

"No, no! The position of her spaceship!" Lone Starr said impatiently.

"She was going in the direction of the Andromeda Strain," King Roland told him.

"I'll bet she's heading for the Carl Sagan Shopping Mall," Barf leaned over and whispered to Lone Starr. "They have the largest pet shop in the galaxy. Maybe if we have time, we could stop and buy me a — "

"We don't have time," Lone Starr said sharply. He looked up at King Roland on the telescreen. "We'll find her," he said slowly, through his teeth, trying to sound like the hero of a space adventure movie.

"Bring her back safely," the King said. "And if you can, try to save the Mercedes."

Meanwhile, aboard the Spaceball Star Cruiser, Sandurz and Dark Helmet kept their eyes on the radar screen. On the screen, the huge green blip was rapidly closing in on the tiny green blip.

"Which one is us again?" Dark Helmet asked.

"The big one. The big one," Sandurz told him.

"I knew that," Dark Helmet said. "I just wanted to make sure *you* weren't mixed up or anything."

"Don't worry, sir. It's going as planned," Sandurz said. "We're closing in on her. Prepare to activate the XG-95 magnetic beam."

"Good," Dark Helmet said. "What's that?"

Sandurz quickly explained it to him. "It's a high-focus electromagnetic spectro-beam that deionizes all matter within its focal range, thereby attracting the deionized matter to the spectro-beam source."

"In other words," Dark Helmet said, scratching his helmet, "what we're talking about here is a very big magnet — right?"

"Yes," Sandurz said quietly. "Essentially, that is what we're talking about, sir."

"Well, activate it then!" Dark Helmet screamed.

"Activate the XG-95 magnetic beam," Sandurz ordered.

Immediately, the beam operator moved his hand forward and pushed two big buttons. "Magnetic beam activated, sir," he called.

Everyone watched on the radar screen as a glowing white magnetic beam burst out from the nose of the Cruiser. It hit the *Honeymoon Coupe*, stopped it in midair, and held it in place.

"That's some big magnet you got there!" Dark Helmet exclaimed. "I'll bet you could use that to keep messages on the refrigerator!"

"Yes, sir," said Sandurz, giving Dark Helmet a funny look, then quickly returning his glance to the radar screen.

The magnetic beam held Princess Vespa's little ship tightly in its grip. Slowly, slowly, it began to pull the *Honeymoon Coupe* back toward the Cruiser.

Chapter 7

As the Princess's *Honeymoon Coupe* was being slowly pulled by the magnetic beam into the mammoth open jaws of the Spaceballs' Cruiser, Lone Starr and his woolly companion rushed to the rescue. Flying at its top speed, the *Eagle Five* drew in close to Vespa's captured ship.

"There's our Princess!" Lone Starr cried.

"Uh-oh," Barf exclaimed, his paws on the throttle. "Spaceballs! They've got her in a magnetic beam. We'd better hurry."

"Okay. Let's move," said Lone Starr, narrowing his eyes the way a movie hero would. "Full throttle."

Barf grabbed the twin throttles tighter and began to push forward. But then he stopped and turned to Lone Starr, who was busy trying to get his eyes a little narrower and maybe get a few masculine creases in his forehead.

"Wait a minute," Barf said. "Why are we risking our lives for a runaway Princess? I know we need the money, but. . . ."

Lone Starr stopped wrinkling his forehead and turned to his sidekick. "Barf, listen. We're not just doing this for money," he said.

"We're not?" Barf exclaimed.

"No," Lone Starr said. "We're doing this for a *lot* of money!"

"Oh. That's different," Barf replied. He began to push forward on the throttles again. "Okay. We're gonna save her. But how? The minute we move in, their radar's gonna spot us."

Lone Starr flashed him a sly grin. "Not if we jam it."

Barf returned the grin. "Good idea." He pulled down a small periscope, sighted through it, and reached for a button on its handle. "Radar about to be . . . jammed." He pushed the button.

A large canister came hurtling out of *Eagle Five*, flying toward the radar dish on the Spaceball Cruiser. *BAAARRROOOOM*. The canister exploded.

A thick, dark, gooey substance splattered onto the radar dish with a loud *plucccccch*. The radar dish slowed, then stopped turning.

Inside the Spaceball Cruiser, the radar operator suddenly jumped to his feet. He pulled off his headphones. They were covered with a thick, wet gook. "Uh . . . sir . . ." he called up to Colonel Sandurz. "I have a problem."

"What is it?" Sandurz called down impatiently.

"It's the radar, sir," the radar operator

said. "It seems to be. . . ." He looked at his headphones. He touched the gook with his finger. He licked his finger. "It seems to be *jammed*!"

"Jammed?" Dark Helmet cried, very alarmed. He hurried over to the radar console. "Let me see that."

Dark Helmet dipped his finger in the dark goo and tasted it. "Raspberry!" he cried angrily. "There's only one man who would dare give me the raspberry!"

"Do you mean — " Sandurz started.

"Yes," Dark Helmet said. "Lone Starr! He knows I'm allergic to raspberries!"

Dark Helmet let go with a powerful sneeze. The sneeze echoed in his helmet for several seconds. He sneezed again. And again. "Everybody knows I'm allergic to raspberries!" he cried.

He sneezed so hard, his visor fell. Now he was sneezing and coughing, then coughing and sneezing. Then just sneezing.

Hidden from the Spaceballs' radar, the *Eagle Five* moved into position above the trapped *Honeymoon Coupe*. "Magnets on!" commanded Lone Starr.

"You don't have to shout. I'm sitting right next to you," Barf complained.

"I'm just trying to make it a little dramatic," Lone Starr said. "Magnets on!" he shouted again.

"Okay, okay. Magnets on," Barf said, pushing several buttons. "We're lined up and locked in on Vespa's ship."

"Well, guess who gets to go down and get her," Lone Starr said with a grin.

"I don't have to guess," his hairy sidekick replied. "I'm already on my way. Although, I wouldn't send a dog out on a night like this."

"I wouldn't go out on a *joke* like that!" Lone Starr said, making a face. But Barf was already on his way.

The hatch door opened in the bottom of the *Eagle Five*, and a Lucite rope ladder dropped down from it. Barf slowly began to lower himself down the ladder. Slowly, carefully he climbed down until he landed on the roof of the *Honeymoon Coupe* with a loud *bump*. (Barf wasn't exactly light on his feet!)

Inside the ship, the worried Princess looked up at the ceiling. "What was that?" she cried.

The bump was followed by a loud knocking on the roof of the ship.

"Never mind that. What is *that*?" Dot cried, shaking so hard she lost a few bolts.

The moon roof slid open, and Barf stuck his hairy head in. He flashed them a big grin. "Hi!"

"YAAAAAIIII!" The Princess and Dot nearly leaped out of the ship.

"Who — who are you?" the Princess managed to ask.

"Barf."

"Not in here, you don't!" Dot screamed.

"No, that's my name," Barf said, still grinning. "Barf."

"Never mind *who* are you," the Princess said. "*What* are you?"

Barf lowered his head a little further into the ship. "I'm a *mawg*," he told them. "Half man, half dog. I'm my own best friend."

He licked his own paw to prove it.

"Ugh," said Vespa, making a face. "Do you have fleas?"

"No. No!" Barf cried defensively. "I just scratch a lot to keep limber. You know, for exercise."

"Well, okay," Vespa said. "You can come in. But don't shed on the carpet. What do you want, anyway?"

Barf lowered himself into the cabin. "Your father hired Captain Lone Starr and me to rescue you. Come on — hop up the ladder."

Dot began to hum excitedly. "Good! We're saved! We're saved! Hurry, darling. Follow the dog."

"That's mawg — *mawg*!" Barf cried, offended.

"But wait — " Vespa said, looking toward the storage hold. "My matched luggage."

"What??" Barf screamed. "Matched luggage! There's no time for matched luggage!"

Vespa's beautiful red lips formed an angry pout. "I'm a Princess. I don't go *anywhere* without matched luggage!"

A few seconds later, Vespa and her faithful droid climbed up the Lucite ladder to the *Eagle Five*. They were followed by Barf, who was having a slightly difficult time climbing since he was weighted down by the Princess's matched luggage.

Barf had a trunk on his back, the handle of one suitcase gripped tightly in his teeth, tote bags hanging from his shoulders, two suitcases under each arm, and a hatbox hanging from his tail! "Ooh, boy — wouldn't you know I have to scratch real bad!" he cried.

Several minutes later, Barf stumbled into the *Eagle Five* and staggered through the rear compartment, falling over Vespa and Dot on his way to the cockpit.

"Are you checking in?" Lone Starr cried when he saw Barf emerge through the curtain.

Barf dropped the suitcase he was carrying in his mouth. "It's Her Highness's matched luggage," he groaned.

"What does she think this is — a Princess Cruise?" Lone Starr exclaimed. He quickly flicked on the intercom. "Now hear this!" he shouted into the microphone. "The minute we get out of here, the first thing we do is dump the matched luggage."

Back in the rear compartment, Vespa picked up a microphone. "Now you hear *this*!" she shouted. "You will not touch my luggage. And furthermore, I want this pigsty cleaned up. All this dust is not good for my sinuses. As a Princess, I cannot allow myself to be rescued in such utter filth."

Lone Starr gripped his microphone tighter in his fist. "Listen, sweetheart," he barked, "on this ship, I don't take orders — I give them!"

Princess Vespa was so enraged, she nearly dropped her microphone. Lone Starr was only three feet in front of her. She was tempted to go up front and really give him a piece of her mind.

But she shouted into the microphone instead. "Sweetheart! How *dare* you speak to me that way. You will address me in the proper manner as Your Royal Highness. I am Princess Vespa, daughter of Roland, King of the Druids."

"I knew it," Lone Starr muttered to Barf. "A Druish Princess!"

"Funny," Barf muttered back, "she doesn't look Druish."

Chapter 8

As the *Eagle Five* sped away with its royal passenger, the Spaceballs pulled the *Honeymoon Coupe* into their Cruiser. Inside the command center of the Cruiser, Dark Helmet, Sandurz, and their lieutenants looked on eagerly, awaiting the moment when they would have Vespa in their clutches.

"Prepare the clutches," Lord Helmet ordered.

"Clutches prepared, sir," one of the Idiots called.

"Turn off the big magnet," Sandurz commanded.

The magnetic beam was turned off. A squad of uniformed Spaceball troopers came trotting in on the double. They quickly surrounded the *Honeymoon Coupe*, their laser rifles at the ready. The leader of the troopers pulled down the ramp of the ship and prepared to enter.

"Hold it! Hold it!" Dark Helmet cried. "I'll handle this personally." He stepped up to the low entrance to the ship. "Now we'll show her who's running this galaxy!"

Dark Helmet slammed down his visor mask and began to stride boldly around the outside of the Princess's spaceship. Immediately, he began to wheeze, and his voice came out of the tight mask choked and tiny.

"So, Princess Vespa" — wheeze, cough — he shouted from behind his mask. "You thought you could outwit the imperious forces of Planet Spaceball."

Dark Helmet bumped into the ship, turned, and walked back in the other direction. "Well, you were wrong. You are now our prisoner. And you will be held hostage until such time as all the air from your planet is transferred to Planet Spaceball."

Lord Helmet walked triumphantly around the ship, gasping for breath. "We don't want to steal your air. We just want to borrow it. Once we have breathed it, we will be happy to return it, and — "

He stopped and opened the door to the *Honeymoon Coupe*. "Hey! She's not in there!"

The troopers all dropped their guns and ran for cover! They knew Dark Helmet could get a little peevish when things went wrong.

The immense chamber grew hushed. Suddenly the voice of the radar operator on the loudspeaker interrupted the silence. "The radar is no longer jammed, sir. We're picking up the outline of a — a Winnebago!"

"Aha!" cried Dark Helmet. "Lone Starr. . . ."

"Follow that Winnebago!" Colonel Sandurz commanded.

"What do I dial for room service?" Princess Vespa asked into her microphone. Dot was busily dusting the cramped rear compartment of the tiny craft.

The *Eagle Five* was speeding away from the Spaceball Cruiser. "Forget about room service. Here comes the Badyear Blimp," Lone Starr said, studying his radar screen. "The Spaceballs are comin' after us."

"We gotta get outta here in a hurry," Barf said.

"Brilliant plan," Lone Starr said sarcastically. "Did you go to college to figure out that one?"

"Well, what's *your* plan?" Barf asked defensively.

"Switch to hyperjets!" Lone Starr or dered.

Barf shrugged. "Okay. Switching to hyperjets." He pushed a few buttons.

Lone Starr switched his intercom back on. "You'd better buckle up back there. We're going into hyperactive."

Three feet behind the cockpit in the rear compartment, Princess Vespa was busy spraying the area with an aerosol can. The can was labeled ROYAL SMELL.

She picked up the microphone and said, "We're going into what?"

"Never mind, honey," came Lone Starr's voice over the speaker. "Just sit down and buckle up."

The Princess's face knotted in fury. "Honey? Who do you think you're talking to? May I remind you. . . ."

She heard a loud click. Lone Starr had flicked off the intercom.

She let out a howl and beat her fists against the wall. "Hate. Hate. Hate. Hate. Hate."

"Don't hold it in, dear," Dot said soothingly. "What do you *really* think of him?"

In the Spaceball Star Cruiser command center, Dark Helmet and his cohorts were in pursuit of the fleeing *Eagle Five*.

"We're closing in on them, sir," the radar operator reported from his console.

"Very good," Sandurz said, eyes on the radar screen. He turned to Lord Helmet. "They'll be ours in less than a minute, sir."

Dark Helmet looked at his watch. "Is that Standard Time?"

"Yes, sir," Sandurz answered.

Dark Helmet looked up and his little face filled with emotion. "Oh, Lone Starr . . ." he said longingly. "I can't wait to make him dead."

"Very well said, sir," Sandurz said, tears forming in his eyes. He turned back to his men. "Prepare for attack."

"On the count of three," Dark Helmet said.

The Spaceball Cruiser was right behind Lone Starr's small craft now and gaining fast.

"One . . ." Dark Helmet called.

The hyperjets on the back of *Eagle Five* began to glow. The Spaceball Cruiser moved closer, closer.

"Two . . ." Dark Helmet called ". . . late!"

In less than a second, *Eagle Five* rocketed off into the star field, leaving Dark Helmet and Sandurz staring into empty space.

"They must have hyperjets on that thing!" cried the astonished Sandurz.

"After them! Catch them! After them!" Dark Helmet screamed.

"Yes, sir," said Sandurz. He yelled into his microphone, "Prepare for light speed."

"No. No. Light speed is too slow!" Lord Helmet protested. "We'll have to go to *ludicrous* speed!"

The astonished Spaceball crew members began to mutter to themselves in surprise and amazement. "Ludicrous speed!"

Sandurz, too, was astonished by the suggestion. "Ludicrous speed!" he cried, gripping the command rail. "We've never gone that fast, sir. I don't know if the ship can take it."

Dark Helmet leaned in menacingly close to his officer. "What's the matter, Colonel Sandurz?" he asked. "Are you *chicken*?"

Chapter 9

"Prepare the ship for ludicrous speed!" Sandurz commanded, the words echoing on loudspeakers throughout the Cruiser.

Was this a wise idea? Or was it a ludicrous idea? They would all soon find out.

"Fasten all seat belts," Sandurz said. "Seal all entrances and exits. Close all shops in the mall. Secure all animals in the zoo."

"Give me that, you wimp!" Dark Helmet cried impatiently, grabbing the microphone from Sandurz's hands. "Now hear this! Ludicrous speed. . . . GO!!"

"But, sir," Sandurz said quietly, "hadn't you better fasten your — "

With an ear-shattering roar, the Spaceball Cruiser leaped into light speed. In the Cruiser's vast windscreen, the sky full of stars became stripes of white light.

"Your seat belt, sir," Sandurz tried to warn his leader. But the roar of the ship drowned out his plea.

The Cruiser jolted forward, moving from

light speed to ridiculous speed. The white stripes were joined by stripes of many colors. The ship began to vibrate violently.

"Ssseat belllt. . . ." Sandurz continued his attempts to warn Dark Helmet.

This time, his voice was drowned out by a warning siren. The ship began to vibrate as if it were inside a blender and someone had pushed PUREE!

LUDICROUS SPEED!

Dark Helmet's eyes bugged out of his head. Outside the windscreen, the stripes weaved themselves together — and formed plaid!

They'd entered the Plaid Zone!

Bathed in eerie plaid light, the crew's faces flattened out as the ship hurtled through space at ludicrous speed.

"Hey — my seat belt . . ." Lord Helmet realized. But it was a little too late. He grabbed onto the command rail as the force of the gravity pull lifted him into the air. His feet fluttered up behind him, kicking at air. His helmet streamed out behind him, pulling back on its elastic straps farther and farther, tighter and tighter.

As his shiny black helmet shot out behind him, Lord Helmet's startled face was revealed. He had patent-leather hair!

"Ohhh, boy," he groaned, holding onto the rail with all his might. "I never did look good in plaid. It's too busy for my figure. . . ."

Meanwhile, traveling at light speed, the

Eagle Five continued to elude its pursuer. Lone Starr and Barf manned (and dogged) the controls, keeping the battered old ship on a steady course.

Suddenly they heard a loud whirr and saw a flash of light go by their windscreen. "What the heck was that?" Barf cried.

"*Spaceball One*," Lone Starr said, narrowing his eyes.

To their surprise, the *Eagle Five* was suddenly bathed in plaid. "Holy moly!" Barf cried. "They've gone to plaid!"

"Plaid was never my color," Lone Starr said, glancing at himself in the mirror. "I always preferred your solids. You know . . . the more masculine pastels. . . ."

Back in *Spaceball One*, Lord Helmet continued to hold on to the command rail for dear life as his body flew up in the air and his helmet was being pulled farther and farther behind him. "You fools! Stop!" he moaned. "We just passed them! Stop!"

"We can't stop! It's too dangerous!" Sandurz shouted above the screaming roar of the engines. "We've got to slow down first!"

"No! No! Stop! Stop!" Dark Helmet screamed.

Shaking his head, Sandurz reluctantly reached for a lever in front of him on the control panel. A light beneath the lever flashed: EMERGENCY STOP — NEVER USE!

Sandurz pushed the lever — and the Cruiser came to a complete halt in less than a second. If a dime had floated in that area of outer space, *Spaceball One* would've stopped on it!

Dark Helmet's eyes opened wide as he realized what was about to happen. "Hoo, boy. Maybe we should've slowed down a little first," he said quietly.

And then his giant helmet snapped back into place, smacked him at full force from behind, and slingshot him up into the air. He sailed about twenty feet across the command center.

The crew turned their heads at the sound of the deafening *crunnnnnch* as their leader landed headfirst in the control panel. His helmet embedded itself in the console. The rest of his body stuck out of the helmet.

Sandurz stepped up to the panel and looked down at the boots of his unfortunate leader. "We've stopped, sir," he said.

"Yes. I noticed," Dark Helmet replied in a tiny whistle of a voice. "Thank you for the information."

"Good thing you were wearing that helmet," Sandurz observed. He stepped around his leader, who remained stuck headfirst in the control console.

"Yes. Good thing," Dark Helmet said weakly.

"What should we do now, sir?" Sandurz asked.

There was a long silence. "Why don't we take a break?" Lord Helmet suggested.

* * *

Far behind the Spaceball Cruiser, Lone Starr began to pull back on the throttle to slow down the *Eagle Five*. "Take her out of hyperactive," he told his hairy sidekick.

"Coming out of hyperactive," Barf said. A smile spread across his face as the ship slowed and the white light outside the window became single stars again. "Congratulations, Boss. We're safe," Barf said. "They overshot us by a year and a half!"

Lone Starr shook Barf's hand. "Okay, let's set a course for Druidia," he said.

"Setting a course for Druidia," the happy mawg said. But his smile quickly faded as the ship began to jerk and toss, and strange, belching noises came from the engine.

"What's that? Did you have pastrami for lunch again?" Lone Starr asked.

"No, Boss," Barf replied. He tapped the fuel gauge. "Uh-oh. We're out of gas."

Lone Starr's mouth dropped open. "Out of gas?"

"We burned it up in hyperactive," Barf told him. "Told you we should've put in more than five bucks worth."

They looked at each other. They looked out at the stars. They weren't moving at all.

"Now what do we do?" Barf asked. "Now what do we do?" He repeated himself to make it all the more dramatic.

Chapter 10

The *Eagle Five* drifted silently in the dark void of space. Barf's face filled with fear and he began to tremble and shake. He did a little scratching. A little more scratching. And then some more trembling.

"Have you got fleas?" Lone Starr asked, reaching for the flea spray.

"No, no!" Barf declared. "Honest I don't! I was just thinking. That's the way I think. Scratching helps me think."

Lone Starr frowned and looked out the front of the ship. His eyes opened wide. He saw something out there. "There's some kind of moon down there," he told his companion. "We've got a tiny bit of fuel left. We've got to try to make an emergency landing."

"You mean a crash landing?" Barf asked.

"I prefer *emergency* landing," Lone Starr said.

"Oh, no." Barf trembled in fear.

"Quick — give me a reading," Lone Starr said.

"Our Father, Who art in Heaven . . ." Barf began.

"Not *that* kind of a reading!" Lone Starr shouted. He picked up the microphone and spoke into the intercom. "Keep your seat belts fastened back there. You okay, Princess?"

Behind the curtain that separated the rear compartment from the cockpit, the Princess grabbed for her microphone. Her hair was completely mussed, she looked terribly disheveled, and her dress was on backward.

"No, I'm not okay, you idiot!" she cried. "I'm okay for a *tossed salad*! But I'm *not* a tossed salad! I'm a Princess! Where did you learn to fly? We've been thrown around back here so hard our — "

CLICK.

Lone Starr turned off the intercom, interrupting her tirade. He turned back to the controls. It wasn't going to be easy to land safely, especially with just a tiny drop of fuel. "Jets off," he said.

"Jets off. Don't like it," Barf replied.

"Rockets reversed," Lone Starr ordered.

"Rockets reversed. Don't like it," Barf replied.

"Gear down," Lone Starr ordered.

"Gear down. Don't like it," came Barf's response.

"*Eagle Five* coming in!" Lone Starr exclaimed.

"*Eagle Five* coming in. Don't like it," Barf replied.

The small ship began to buck and rattle. Its passengers were jerked from side to side, tossed violently back and forth as Lone Starr fought to control it. Finally, *Eagle Five* lurched to a jarring stop.

It took a while to stop bouncing and shaking. Then Lone Starr announced, "The *Eagle* has landed."

He looked over at his sidekick. Barf's ears covered his eyes. Slowly, Barf peeked out.

"I like it," he said.

In the back compartment, the Princess and Dot tried to pull themselves together after the violent, jarring landing.

Dot opened one eye, then the other. "Is it over?" she asked.

"Yes," Vespa told her. She pulled off her seat belt, slammed it angrily to the floor, and headed for the curtain that separated them from the cockpit.

"Where are you going?" Dot asked weakly.

The Princess shook her fist at the curtain. "I'm going to tell him off once and for all."

"No. Wait a minute," Dot called to her. "We'll need him to get us out of here. Besides" — a smile formed on her pretty mechanical face — "he's got a nice voice. He could be cute."

The Princess sneered. "Cute! I know these space bums. They're all alike — fat, ugly, beer-swilling pigs!"

On the other side of the curtain, Lone Starr unbuckled his seat belt and prepared to go back and face the Princess. "She called me an idiot!" he exclaimed angrily. "I'm going back there and — "

"Hold it!" Barf held him back. "Wait till you see what she looks like. She's — "

"I *know* what she looks like," Lone Starr interrupted, shoving Barf out of his way. "If you've seen one princess, you've seen them all — buck-toothed, knock-kneed, horse-faced space dogs!"

He walked up to the stained curtain, but before he could open it, Princess Vespa yanked it open from the other side.

"Now, listen, you — " she started, fury in her eyes. But she stopped, stunned by Lone Starr's rugged good looks.

"You listen — " Lone Starr started to say. But his stubbled jaw dropped open. Vespa's beauty left him speechless.

For a few seconds, they stared silently at each other.

Lone Starr was the first to recover. "You listen," he said, softer than before. "On this ship, you are to refer to me as *idiot* — not *you captain*. I mean . . . uh. . . . You know what I mean."

"And you are not to call me *you*," the Princess replied, not as angrily as she had started out. "You'll never address me as *you*. You will address me as 'Your Royal Highness.' "

Lone Starr felt his anger coming back. "You are a royal pain — " he started.

"Hold it!" Barf interrupted. He made a

"T" sign with his paws. "Time out. May I make a small suggestion?"

"What's your suggestion?" Lone Starr asked.

"You're both crazy," Barf said.

"That's a suggestion?" Vespa exclaimed.

"Listen to me," Barf said, sounding worried. "Any minute now, the Spaceballs are going to make a major U-turn, head back here, and make us all dead."

"That's a suggestion?" Vespa repeated.

"He's right," Lone Starr said quickly, realizing there was little time to waste. "Let's get out of here."

"Wait!" Vespa cried, grabbing his arm. "My things!"

Lone Starr backed away angrily. "Now, listen, Your Royal Highness," he said, making the words *Your Royal Highness* sound like some kind of gum disease. "Take only what you need to survive."

A few minutes later, they stepped out onto the barren Moon of Vega; into a drab vista of endless gray rocks, barren sand dunes, and deep black craters. The land stretched empty, silent, and still as far as the eye could see.

The Princess, walking slowly, reluctantly, led the way, carrying a tote bag and a matching hatbox. She was followed by the faithful Dot, pulling an airline luggage hauler that contained two overstuffed matching suitcases.

Lone Starr and Barf followed, straining and struggling to carry a huge matching steamer trunk. "What the heck is in this thing?" Lone Starr asked Barf. "It weighs a ton."

"Let's set it down, Boss. Please!" Barf wheezed.

They set the trunk down on the sand. Lone Starr bent down and snapped open the top. Then he reached into the trunk and pulled out a large white object — a hair dryer bigger than a bicycle!!

"Your Royal Highness, what's this?" Lone Starr asked wearily. "I said take only what you need to survive."

"It's my industrial-strength hair dryer," the Princess snapped. "And I *can't* live without it!"

Lone Starr frowned and shook his head. "Okay, Princess, that's it. The fairy tale is over. Welcome to real life. You want this hot air machine? You carry it!" He tossed it to the ground at her feet.

Vespa jumped back. "My father is paying you a lot of money," she shrieked. "You pick that up!"

"*You* pick it up!" Lone Starr yelled.

The Princess raised her head haughtily in royal disapproval. "How dare you! You insolent peasant! Nobody talks to me that way! Nobody!"

Lone Starr's eyes flared angrily. He was ready for a good fight. She had been asking for it ever since he rescued her. "Look at her," he said. "Those flashing eyes, those flushed cheeks, those trembling lips. . . . You know something, Princess?"

"I'm beautiful when I'm angry?" she suggested.

"No. Ugly as a goat," he told her.

"That does it!" Vespa screamed. "You and your dog are fired!"

"Mawg! I'm a *mawg*!" Barf whined.

Still pulling the luggage carrier, Dot moved over to the Princess. "Don't fire him now. He's rescuing us," she said. "Wait until he saves our lives. *Then* fire him!"

"Good plan," the Princess said.

"May I make a suggestion?" Barf said, sounding desperate.

"We're crazy?" Lone Starr and Vespa replied in unison.

"No. It's gonna be pitch-dark soon. We've gotta find a place to camp for the night. My dogs are killing me!"

"He's right. Let's move on," Lone Starr said, surveying the horizon.

Leaving the trunk and king-size hair dryer behind, they started off over the barren terrain, walking slowly into the darkness, into the scary unknown. . . .

Chapter 11

Aboard *Spaceball One,* Lord Helmet paced the command module as his crew desperately searched the skies for Lone Starr and the *Eagle Five.* "Any sign of them yet?" he called to the radar operator.

"No, Lord Helmet," came the reply. "They don't show up on the scanner. It's all black, sir. Nothing but blackness."

Lord Helmet walked down to the scanner. "All black? Well, try turning it on, you idiot! You might see a little better."

"Whoops. Sorry, sir." The radar operator reached up and turned on the scanner. "Still no sign of them, sir."

"Well, keep looking." Lord Helmet returned to the bridge.

The loudspeaker crackled to life suddenly with an important announcement: "Attention. Attention. There are still tickets left for the three-ring circus from Saturn that will be touring the ship from May to December."

"We've *got* to find Lone Starr and the Princess," Lord Helmet said. "This is putting me in a bad mood."

"Pardon me, sir," Sandurz interrupted. "I have an idea." Sandurz walked over to the Spaceball video technician. "Do we have a videocassette of *Spaceballs — The Movie?*"

"I'll look, sir." The video technician got up from his console and pulled open a sliding panel, revealing a wall of videocassettes. "We have all the Mel Brooks movies here, Colonel Sandurz," he said.

He ran his hand quickly across the shelf, looking for the cassette of *Spaceballs*. "You sure you wouldn't rather watch *Blazing Saddles*? It's a riot. I love the scene where they're sitting around the campfire and — "

"Wait a minute!" Lord Helmet called down from the bridge. "There *can't* be a cassette of *Spaceballs* yet! We're still in the middle of *living* it!"

"That's true, sir," Sandurz said. "But there's been a new breakthrough in home video marketing."

Dark Helmet's little face filled with surprise. "There has?"

"Yes. Instant cassettes. They're out in stores before the movie is finished."

"Wow!" Dark Helmet didn't really understand what Sandurz was talking about. "What won't they think of next?"

The crew member popped the *Spaceballs* cassette into the VCR. The FBI warning appeared on the screen, followed by the beginning of the movie and the words "Once upon a time warp. . . ."

"No, no no. Skip it ahead. Skip it ahead!" Dark Helmet cried impatiently.

The crew member pushed FAST FORWARD. The tape spun ahead as static filled the screen. "Try now!" Dark Helmet called. "Quick search!"

Everyone watched the screen. Once again, in very speeded-up motion, they saw the *Spaceball One* come out of ludicrous speed, and Dark Helmet go flying helmet-first into the control console.

"No! No! Keep going!" Dark Helmet cried. "Good lord — how embarrassing!"

The technician fast-forwarded the movie some more. "Let's try here," Dark Helmet ordered. The technician pushed PLAY.

Dark Helmet stepped forward to get a closer look. On the screen, Dark Helmet stepped forward to get a closer look at a video screen. He moved closer. The image of himself on the screen moved closer. Closer. Closer. Soon, the two identical Dark Helmets were nose to nose.

"What's going on here?" Dark Helmet demanded.

At the exact same time, the Dark Helmet on the video screen asked, "What's going on here?"

"What am I looking at? When does this happen?" Lord Helmet cried.

The Dark Helmet on the screen said the

exact same words at the exact same time.

"Now. You're looking at now, sir," Sandurz said. And a Sandurz on the screen said those very same words. "Everything that happens now is happening now."

Dark Helmet's mouth dropped open. He was thinking hard, trying to understand this. "Now?" He sounded very confused. "What happened to *then*?"

"We passed *then*," Sandurz told him.

"When?"

"Just now. We're at *now* now," Sandurz said.

"Then go back to *then*," Dark Helmet said.

"When?" Sandurz asked.

"Now," Dark Helmet replied.

"Now?" Sandurz asked. "Now?" the Sandurz on the screen asked.

"Not now — then," the two Dark Helmets said. "Go back to then."

"I can't," the two Sandurzes said.

"Why?"

"We missed it," Sandurz told him.

"When?"

"Just now," Sandurz said.

"Wait!" Dark Helmet cried. "When will then be now?"

"Soon."

"Not now?" Dark Helmet asked.

"No."

"When?" Dark Helmet asked.

"Now," Sandurz said.

Dark Helmet's eyes rolled around in his

head, and his tongue hung down from his mouth. The great leader was terribly confused.

As they watched the video screen, the scene suddenly changed. They found themselves staring at the barren, rocky terrain of some distant moon. The Princess stepped into the scene, followed by Dot, Lone Starr, and Barf. All of them were carrying luggage.

"We've done it!" the radio operator cried. "We've identified their location!"

Dark Helmet's eyes were still rolling around in his head. "Where?"

"It's the Moon of Vega," the radio operator announced.

"Good work!" Sandurz cried happily. "Set a course and prepare for our arrival."

"When?" Dark Helmet asked weakly.

"Nineteen-hundred hours, sir," the radio operator announced.

"What?" Dark Helmet uttered in total confusion.

"By high noon tomorrow, they will be our prisoners, sir," Sandurz told him.

"Who?" Dark Helmet asked.

Chapter 12

The Moon of Vega was not one of the big tourist attractions in the universe. One reason for this was the interesting and beautiful scenery. There wasn't any.

There was just rocks and desert, followed by more desert and an occasional rock.

Another reason why most folks preferred Disney World to the Moon of Vega was the temperature. In the off-season, it went up to about 200 degrees in the daytime, then slid down to about 20 below zero at night.

There was no in-season.

Our heroes were not aware of this information. They were just pleased to have escaped from the clutches of the ruthless Spaceballs and to have landed safely on firm ground. They set up camp on a high, flat dune under a sky full of twinkling stars.

Barf fell asleep immediately, comfy on a big rubber doughnut that had the words INFLATO DOGGIE BED stenciled on its side. Across from him, Dot sat motionless on the ground. A little orange sign on her shoulder flicked on and off. It said: SLEEP MODE. From across the way, Lone Starr could hear her electronic, digital snoring. . . . "Beep-*BLEEP*. Beep-*BLEEP*."

A short distance away, Princess Vespa sat on a gray boulder and looked up wistfully at the vast night sky. She shivered, rubbing her arms to get warm.

Lone Starr walked over quietly, his long legs taking him to her in just a few strides. He pulled off his tattered leather flight jacket and slipped it around her shoulders.

"No, thank you," she said. "I'm perfectly all right."

She began to take off the jacket, but Lone Starr put it back on. "Keep it," he said softly. "Blue isn't exactly the most appealing skin color."

"You say the sweetest things," she said sarcastically. But then her tone softened and she looked up at him, her beautiful brown eyes filled with genuine concern. "Won't you be cold?"

"Nah," Lone Starr said, narrowing his eyes and trying to get those heroic creases in his forehead. "Cold never bothers me." He began to shiver. He hoped she couldn't hear his teeth chattering.

Vespa gazed up at the sky. "I can't seem to find Druidia," she said.

Lone Starr picked a direction and pointed. "It's there," he said.

"Where?" She leaned back to look and nearly fell off the rock.

"Right up there," he said, pointing in a different direction. "That bright blue one. See?"

"Oh, yes," the Princess said, a smile curving her luscious red lips. "I see. It's so far away. . . ."

"Don't worry. I'll get you there," Lone Starr said, shivering too hard to sound as confident as he'd intended.

"Which one is yours?" she asked.

"Who knows?"

She looked up at him in surprise. "You don't know where you're from?"

"Not really," Lone Starr said with a shrug. "I was found on the doorstep of a monastery. Somewhere in the Ford Galaxy."

"Didn't the monks tell you who your parents were?" Vespa asked.

"They couldn't," he told her. "They took a vow of silence. All I've got is this." From beneath his shirt, Lone Starr pulled out a tarnished silver medallion. "It was around my neck when they found me," he told her. "I've worn it there ever since."

"You should wash it sometime," she said.

"The medallion?"

"No. Your neck," she said. But she immediately regretted her harshness. She cradled the medallion in her hand. On one side she could make out strange hieroglyphic writing. "What does it say?"

"I don't know," Lone Starr said, sounding really choked up. She was pulling a bit too hard on the medallion chain. "I've taken it to every wise man in the universe. But nobody can tell me what it means."

She pulled a little harder to get a better look. Their faces came together. They stared into each other's eyes.

"I — I — " Lone Starr struggled to find the right words. "I — I can't breathe!" He took the medallion from her hand and replaced it under his shirt.

The moment was lost. They looked up at the stars again. "So how come you ran away from your wedding?" Lone Starr asked.

"If you must know, I wasn't in love with the groom," she said, not looking at him.

"Then why were you going to marry him?"

"Because I'm a princess and I have to marry a prince. I have a duty to my father and my planet." She stopped for a moment. She seemed to be trying to keep herself from crying. "I really must go back," she said. "I shouldn't have run away. I realize now that love is one luxury that a princess cannot afford."

Lone Starr moved a little closer. "You're probably right."

"I know now that I must learn to live without love," she said softly.

"I guess so . . ." Lone Starr said, moving a little closer and putting a hand on her shoulder.

"Besides, love isn't that important," she said.

"Naah, it isn't," Lone Starr quickly agreed.

He pulled her close. They began to melt into each other's arms. Their lips touched.

WHOOOP! WHOOOOOP! WHOOOOOP!

A siren wailed from Dot's head. A red light began to flash on her chest. She came running over, pulled the Princess away, and turned angrily to Lone Starr. "We'll have none of that, Mr. Make-Out!"

Lone Starr raised his hands and backed away. "Okay. Okay. Let's all get some sleep. We've gotta get moving before dawn."

"Before dawn?" Princess Vespa whined. "Why so early?"

"We're in the middle of the desert," Lone Starr told her. "We won't get very far once that blazing sun gets overhead."

As they walked off in different directions to their sleeping areas, Vespa cast a last, lingering look at him. Lone Starr cast a lingering look, too — at his jacket. He *really* wanted it back. . . .

By midmorning the sun was a blistering hot yellow ball. The heat sizzled down and was reflected back up by the white-hot desert sand.

As our four pitiful heroes staggered across the burning sands, they abandoned Vespa's luggage piece by piece. But even with a lighter load, the heat was unbearable, the journey slow and exhausting.

Up they climbed to the top of a steep sand dune. Lone Starr was in the lead, his face red and sweat-soaked, his parched lips gasping, "Water . . . water!"

Barf followed, his tongue down to his knees, panting quickly like a dog, gasping, "Water . . . water!"

Dot followed behind him, also exhausted, ready to drop, gasping, "Oil . . . oil!"

She was followed by the exhausted Princess, gasping, "Room service . . . room service!"

Chapter 13

All eyes were on the telescreen as *Spaceball One* closed in on the Moon of Vega. Finally, the radar technician made the announcement Lord Helmet was waiting to hear. "Picking up life forms in Vector 78, sir," he reported. "Three humans and a droid. They're alive but unconscious."

Lord Helmet rubbed his gloved hands together gleefully. "Alive but unconscious! Just the way I like my enemies! Ha ha!"

"Ready the landing party to pick up the prisoners," Colonel Sandurz ordered. "We'll go in the sand cruiser, sir."

But Dark Helmet didn't hear him. He was moaning in anticipation of finally capturing his longtime foe. "Ohh, Lone Starr," he sighed. "Ohhh, Lone Starr, Lone Starr. . . . I'm going to make you so unbelievably dead!"

On the sizzling sands of the Moon of Vega, Lone Starr and his three companions already appeared to be dead. But they were only unconscious, overcome by exhaustion and the stifling heat.

With Lord Helmet and his ruthless Spaceballs closing in on them, however, they were as good as dead. Luckily for our heroes, Dark Helmet was not the first one to find them.

From out of the sand, a little fuzzy head wearing a sand-colored hood popped up, its pawlike hands scratching a path for itself. "Dink," the little creature called out meekly, spotting the large, unmoving creatures in front of it. "Dink dink," it called out a little more bravely.

"Dink dink?" Another small, hooded creature popped up from the sand. It was followed by three others. "Dink dink."

"Dink dink dink!"

The Dinks were about three feet tall. They all wore identical robes tied with a tiny rope and open-pawed sandals. They looked like furry little monks.

"Dink dink? Dink!"

"Dink dink dink dink dink."

They chattered excitedly among themselves, worried about the four unconscious figures in the sand. "Dink dink dink dink dink!"

They formed a circle around Lone Starr and his companions, and trying to revive them, began to give them water from their canteens.

"Hey, thanks, little guy," Barf said gratefully, gulping down the water the Dink offered.

"Thank you, thank you," the grateful Princess said.

"Glug glug glug." Dot gratefully lapped up the quart of oil the friendly little creatures poured down her throat.

Next, they tried to revive Lone Starr. Slowly, he opened his eyes, shielded them from the sun, and looked around. "Hey — where are we? Disneyland?"

"They saved us," Barf told his still-dazed boss.

"Are they chipmunks — or what?" Lone Starr asked.

"Dink dink dink dink."

"Yeah. Right." He slowly climbed to his feet.

The Dinks led Lone Starr and his weary companions off across the sand. After a while, they came to a winding stone staircase that led deep into the ground. Down they went, following the chattering Dinks until they arrived on a flat stone floor in a dark anteroom of some sort.

"Where are we? What is this place?" Vespa asked, looking around the mysterious structure.

"Dink dink dink dink dink dink dink," the Dink leader explained in great detail.

"Thank you," the Princess replied.

"Glad you cleared that up," Barf added.

The anteroom led to an immense cavern

carved out of stone. Lone Starr and the others stared in disbelief. The enormous chamber appeared to be a mile high with tall white pillars reaching to the ceiling. A marble altar, bathed in bright light, stood at the far end of the cavern. And sitting on the high altar was a twenty-foot-tall Buddha-like statue with gleaming ruby-red eyes; huge, pointed ears; and nostrils that breathed smoke.

The Dinks bowed their heads solemnly. The Dink leader gestured for Lone Starr and his companions to step closer to the statue.

"Now what's going to happen?" Vespa whispered.

"Don't ask and maybe it won't . . ." Lone Starr whispered back.

As Lone Starr reluctantly moved closer, a ball of flame burst from the statue's mouth.

"Woof woof woof!" The frightened Barf forgot himself and began to bark like a dog.

"SILENCE!"

The booming voice of the statue echoed deafeningly off the cavern walls.

"Who DARES enter the sacred and AWESOME presence of the everlasting Know-It-All?" the statue roared.

"Everlasting Know-It-All?" Lone Starr muttered to himself. "It *can't* be. He's been dead for a thousand years!"

"Don't tell *him* that!" Vespa whispered. "Who is he, anyway?"

"Who is he?" Dot asked.

"Who?" Barf repeated.

"It's . . . Yogurt!" Lone Starr exclaimed, his voice filled with awe.

"Yogurt!" Barf, Dot, and Vespa exclaimed in unison.

"Hey! You hoida me?" Yogurt emerged from the folds of the statue's robes. He was a cute three-foot-tall version of the statue.

"Heard of you!" Lone Starr exclaimed. "Who hasn't heard of Yogurt?"

"Yogurt the Wise," Vespa said, smiling.

"Yogurt the All-Powerful," Dot added, whirring with excitement.

"Yogurt the Magnificent!" Barf said.

Yogurt gave them a little wave. He looked embarrassed. "Please, please. I'm just plain Yogurt."

"But weren't you the leader of the Red-Eye Knights and the possessor of the Force?" Barf asked.

"No, no. That was Alec Guinness," Yogurt told him. He flashed them a wise and knowing grin. "I am the keeper of a greater magic," he said proudly. "I possess a power known throughout the universe as . . . the Schwartz!"

With these astounding words, Yogurt held up his right hand, revealing a silver ring on his middle finger. A dazzling silver light circled the ring.

"The *Schwartz*!" our heroes cried in unison. The light was so dazzling, they looked away.

"Don't be afraid," Yogurt told them. "The Schwartz is in the service of the pure and the brave and the good and the cute."

The Dinks had gathered around Yogurt. They began chattering noisily and tugging at his sleeves. "Dink dink dink! Dink dink?"

"Oh, of course I'll introduce you," Yogurt said, slapping the side of his head. "Where are my manners?" He gestured to the excited little creatures who surrounded him. "These are my Dinks. I couldn't live without them. They're my little helpers."

He began to introduce them one by one. "This guy is Rinky Dink. Next to him is Blinky Dink. And that's Stinky Dink. Over here, we got Pinky, Finky, and Winky."

Winky winked at the Princess.

"What is this place?" Lone Starr asked. "What do you do here?"

"What do we do here?" Yogurt repeated. "I'll tell you what we do here. Merchandising."

"What's that?" Barf asked, scratching his head.

"You know . . . merchandising," Yogurt said. "First they make the movie. Then they make the book about the movie. Then they make a million things with the movie's name on it. C'mere, I'll show you."

Yogurt led them across the wide cavern to a display shelf. The shelf was filled with all kinds of *Spaceballs* products.

"Here. Look," Yogurt said, holding up items one by one. "See? A *Spaceballs* coloring book . . . a *Spaceballs* lunch box . . . T-shirts . . . even dolls. Here. Take a look at our latest doll — me!"

He held up a very cute little doll of himself. "I'm adorable — and I talk," he said, smiling proudly. "I'll show you."

He pulled a string on the back of the Yogurt doll, and in a squeaky little doll voice, it said, "May the Schwartz be with you!"

Yogurt grinned and gestured to all the stuff on the shelf. "Let's face it, folks," he said. "Toys are us!"

Chapter 14

Into the heat of the Vegan desert marched Dark Helmet and his Spaceballs, continuing their ruthless search for Princess Vespa. They moved slowly over the blazing sand, their eyes peeled for any sign of Vespa and the others.

As Dark Helmet tried to shield his eyes from the blinding sun, Sandurz came running up to him. "We've reported to President Skroob that the Princess is somewhere in the Sands of Vega, sir," Sandurz told him.

"And what did President Skroob say?" Dark Helmet asked, trying to find some shade in the depths of his helmet.

"President Skroob said to comb the desert and to leave no stone unturned," Sandurz reported.

"Okay, men — comb the desert!" Dark Helmet commanded.

Immediately, the Spaceball troopers pulled out giant black Ace combs, the size of a city bus, and began to comb the desert with them.

They combed and combed. All that combing put a nice wave in the desert and a neat part on the left — but it didn't turn up any sign of Princess Vespa.

"Okay, men," Dark Helmet called. "Start turning over stones!"

The troopers put down their combs, bent down, and began turning over stones. A few hours later, Sandurz, looking disappointed and exhausted, reported to Dark Helmet. "There's no sign of them, sir. We left no stone unturned."

"Oh, yeah?" Dark Helmet cried. "What about that one?" He took two steps, bent down, and turned over a stone.

Beneath the stone lay a golden bracelet. Dark Helmet smiled triumphantly and picked it up. "See? Her bracelet." He held it up and read the inscription: *To Princess Vespa from King Daddy — Happy Purim.*

Dark Helmet waved the bracelet in Sandurz's weary face. "They've got to be somewhere nearby. Keep searching!"

The Princess and her companions *were* nearby, feeling safe and comfortable in Yogurt's underground cavern. As Vespa, Dot, and Barf rested from their exhausting journey through the Vegan desert, Lone Starr went off with Yogurt to take instruction in using the Schwartz.

Lone Starr towered over Yogurt. He was at least three feet taller than the little guy. But Yogurt's small size was misleading. His wisdom was large and he held enormous powers.

Lone Starr pulled out the medallion he wore around his neck and held it down to Yogurt. "It's a mystery," Lone Starr said. "None of the wise men could tell me what it means."

"Wise men? What do they know?" Yogurt scoffed. "They're all a bunch of dummies. Let me take a look."

He reached up for the medallion. Then, to get a better look at it, he stood up. He had been walking on his knees all along! His little green shoes were attached to his knees with rubber bands. His full-length robe was now knee-length, revealing bare, bony legs, little white ankle socks, and worn bedroom slippers.

"Oy! What a pleasure to stand up," Yogurt sighed. "It's hard to work on your knees at my age."

"Yogurt, how old are you?" Lone Starr asked, still startled by Yogurt's new height.

"I'm eight-five . . . hundred . . . and forty-two years young," Yogurt said proudly. "I don't look a day over eighty-five hundred — do I?"

He held the medallion up close to his face and began to examine it carefully. "Hmmm . . . let's see here. No wonder they couldn't figure it out. This is written in the oldest language known to man."

"What's that?" Lone Starr asked. "Greek? Sanskrit? Latin?"

"Older," Yogurt said.

"Older than Latin?"

"Yes," Yogurt told him. "It's *Pig* Latin!"

"Can you read it? What does it say?" Lone Starr asked eagerly.

A mysterious look crossed Yogurt's face. "I can't tell you now. It shall be revealed to you at the proper time."

"When is that?" Lone Starr asked.

"Just before the end of this book."

Lone Starr looked disappointed. But Yogurt pulled him in front of the enormous Yogurt statue. "Let's get back to your Schwartz training," he said. "Concentrate and try again."

Lone Starr stepped back and raised his right hand. On his middle finger, he was now wearing Yogurt's silver ring. "Okay," he said, looking skeptically at the ring, "but I still don't see how I can lift that big statue with this little ring."

Yogurt's face creased into a wise and knowing smile. "Never underestimate the power of the Schwartz," he said quietly.

Lone Starr pointed his ring finger toward the statue, closed his eyes, and concentrated with all his might. The ring began to glow. A few seconds later, the huge statue began to rise.

"I can't believe it!" Lone Starr cried, opening his eyes, seeing the statue float up into the air. "The Schwartz — it's working!"

At that moment, Barf came running in excitedly. "Hey, Boss, I'm — uh — "

Lone Starr turned to look at his sidekick and —

CRAAAAAASSSH!

"Oooh, wow!" Yogurt screamed. "Ooh, boy! Woof! Wow! Ouch!"

"Oh. I'm terribly sorry," Barf said. "That big statue seems to have fallen onto your little foot."

"Can we talk later?" Yogurt screamed. "Get it off! Get it off me!"

"Come on, Barf. On three, let's lift," Lone Starr said, bending down to get a grip on the immense statue. They tried to lift it off Yogurt's foot, but it wouldn't budge. "It's no use," Lone Starr said, still straining to lift it.

"Use the Schwartz, Lone Starr!" Yogurt screamed. "Use the Schwartz!"

"Hey. Good idea!" Lone Starr said, suddenly remembering the ring on his finger. He waved Barf back and then pointed the ring at the statue, concentrating with all his might.

The ring began to glow. The statue slowly began to rise. Yogurt pulled his foot out. "That's better!" Yogurt cried. "That's better! That's — "

CRAAAAAASSSH!

"That's not so good," Yogurt said, shaking his head. But this time the statue had missed his foot by half an inch.

"Look at my foot!" he wailed. "It looks like a spatula! I knew I should never have gotten off my knees!"

Chapter 15

Night fell on the desert of Vega, turning the sands cold and white. Dark Helmet and his troopers huddled in disappointment and defeat. "It's no use, sir," Sandurz said sadly. "We've searched everywhere."

"Wait!" Dark Helmet cried, holding up a hand for silence. He seemed to be listening to some sort of invisible signal. "I feel it. . . . I feel the presence of the Schwartz!" he exclaimed.

"The Schwartz!" his men all repeated in awe.

Dark Helmet turned around and began walking toward a low dune behind them. "It's coming from there," he said, still listening. "Somewhere down there."

Sandurz walked up to where Dark Helmet was pointing. He brushed the sand away. Two doors came into view. On each door was a circle with a big Y carved inside it.

"You're right, sir," Sandurz said, impressed. "There *is* a secret entrance here.

And look at the insignia on the doors."

"Y for Yogurt," Dark Helmet frowned. "I *hate* Yogurt. Even with fruit on the bottom!"

"I'll call for the attack squad, sir," Sandurz said eagerly.

"No!" Dark Helmet held him back. "We can't go in there. Yogurt has the Schwartz. It's too powerful."

"But your ring — " Sandurz protested. "What's that — chopped liver? Don't you have the Schwartz, too?"

"Yes," Dark Helmet told him, "but he's got the upside. . . . I got the downside."

"Then how are we going to go in and get her?" Sandurz asked.

Dark Helmet thought for a moment. Then he had an idea. He threw back his head and uttered a long, evil laugh so that everyone would know that he'd had an idea. "We will not go in there," he said mysteriously.

"What?" Sandurz asked, confused.

"She will come out to *us*!" Dark Helmet declared, and did a little more evil laughing just for the heck of it.

Then he lowered his helmet visor, raised the ring, pointing it toward the two doors, and began to concentrate.

In the dark warmth of the cavern bedchambers, everyone slept. Dot snored her mechanical snores, her SLEEP MODE sign blinking on and off. Nearby, Princess Vespa slept peacefully, too.

Suddenly, a familiar voice entered the Princess's dreams. "Vespa, my child — where are you?"

Vespa blinked and sat up, wide awake. "Daddy? Is that you?" she called softly.

"Vespa, it's your father, King Roland," the voice called. "Come to me."

Vespa's heart began to pound. "Daddy, I hear you. I hear you. Where are you?"

"Follow my voice," the voice of King Roland said. "Come to me. Come to me. Hurry it up, will ya?"

The Princess eagerly leaped from the bed. Following the sound of her father's voice, she opened the door to the bedchamber, headed down the silent hallways, and then up the steps to the front entrance.

Suddenly, Dot's alarm began to buzz. Her SLEEP MODE sign went off. Her eyes slid open. She looked around the dark bedchamber. Her gears began to whirr noisily as she realized the Princess was missing.

In the moonlit desert outside the cavern entrance, King Roland stood in all his royal splendor. He waited, a frown on his round face, until he heard the sound of a bolt being slid back inside. Then he smiled as the doors opened and Princess Vespa stepped out.

"Daddy! It's really you!" she cried happily, unable to believe her eyes.

"Come to me," King Roland said, beaming back at her, opening his arms wide.

The Princess, tears of happiness running

down her cheeks, began to run toward her father.

Dot moved quickly through the cavern and stopped just before the outer doorways. She reached for two buttons on her side. One was labeled NORMAL VISION. The other was labeled ABNORMAL VISION.

She pushed ABNORMAL VISION. Her eyes began to glow with an infrared light. To her horror, she immediately saw that the Princess was not running to her father. Inside the welcoming figure of the king was Dark Helmet!

"No, Vespa! No!" Dot called out. "He's not really — "

A Spaceball trooper stepped out of the darkness and put a hand over Dot's mouth. He pulled open a compartment in her back and yanked out her battery pack. Dot froze in place, silent and lifeless.

Princess Vespa leaped into the king's waiting arms. Instantly, he transformed back into the evil figure of Dark Helmet.

"Ha-ha! Fooled ya!" he said.

Chapter 16

Too late, Lone Starr, Barf, and the Dinks came running out to rescue the Princess. They were just in time to see the Spaceball Star Cruiser blasting off with Vespa and Dot aboard.

"We've got to go after them!" Lone Starr cried.

"Good thinking, Boss," Barf agreed.

Yogurt loaned them a can of gasoline, which Barf quickly poured into the tank of the flying Winnebago.

"Remember — get to a gas station as fast as you can," Yogurt warned. "That gallon won't get you very far. You've got a long way to go to Spaceball City. And here. . . ." He reached into the pocket of his robe, pulled something out, and tossed it to Lone Starr.

"What's this?" Lone Starr asked, turning it over in his hand. "Some sort of secret weapon?"

"No," Yogurt said. "It's just in case you

get hungry. It's a fortune cookie. Be sure to open it before you eat it."

Lone Starr looked puzzled, but he stuffed the cookie into his pocket. "Well, we're on our way. Will we ever see you again?"

"Who knows?" Yogurt shrugged. "Here's hoping we'll all meet again in the sequel — *Spaceballs Two, The Search for More Money!*"

Yogurt stretched out his hand to shake Lone Starr's. "Good-bye, Lone Starr. And good luck."

Lone Starr shook Yogurt's hand solemnly. When he opened his hand, Yogurt's silver ring was on his finger. "Hey, Yogurt — the ring of the Schwartz. It's on my finger."

"Wear it in good health," Yogurt said. "It's you. It's really you." Then he disappeared into the depths of his mystical cavern.

Dark Helmet, laughing triumphantly all the way, guided *Spaceball One* with its two prisoners on board to his planet's capital, Spaceball City. Immediately after landing at Spaceball International, Vespa and Dot were dragged into the largest of the white Ping-Pong ball buildings.

There, in President Skroob's office, Dark Helmet began to put the next part of his ruthless plan into operation.

"Get her father, King Roland, on the televiewer," Dark Helmet commanded.

A few seconds later, the surprised face of

the King appeared on the wallscreen. Roland's face quickly turned from surprise to anger. "Helmet, you fiend — what's going on?" he screamed. "What are you doing to my daughter?"

King Roland could see that his daughter the Princess had been strapped down to a tilted operating-room gurney. Beside her stood a doctor wearing a light green operating smock, mask, and cap. The doctor held a scalpel close to Vespa's terrified face.

"Greetings, King Roland," Dark Helmet said to the image on the wallscreen. "I'd like you to meet Dr. Philip Schlotkin. He's the greatest nose-job man in the universe. He's about to operate on your lovely daughter."

King Roland's eyes grew wide. His mouth dropped open in bewilderment. "Nose job? I don't understand," he exclaimed. "She's already had a nose job. It was her Sweet Sixteen present."

Dark Helmet's thin lips curled in an evil grin. "No. It's not what you think," he told the King. "It's a lot worse. If you don't tell us the combination to your planet's air shield . . . Dr. Schlotkin is going to give her back her *old* nose!"

"No! No! Please! No!" Vespa and her father screamed together in unison.

"Yes!" Dark Helmet gleefully insisted.

"All right. I'll tell. I'll tell!" King Roland cried.

But Vespa courageously raised her head

and shouted, "No, Daddy — no! You mustn't tell. What is my nose compared to the lives of millions of our people?!"

Her words made the King pause and think. "I guess you're right, my dear," he said finally. "I'll certainly miss your new nose. But I'll never tell them the combination to the air shield! Never!"

Hearing the King's defiant words, Dr. Schlotkin pulled the green mask off his mouth, and turned to Dark Helmet. "If you don't need me, can I go back to the golf course now?"

"Yeah, yeah. Get outta here," Dark Helmet said, disgustedly waving him away.

Dr. Schlotkin picked up his golf clubs from under the operating-room gurney and left. A few seconds later, the door swung open and in bounded President Skroob. "Well, Helmet? What's the combination?" he asked, rubbing his hands together eagerly.

"Well . . . er . . . uh . . ." Dark Helmet stammered.

"Your *fershlugginer* nose-job plan didn't work, did it!" President Skroob shouted. "I told you it wouldn't. I told you no one would pick a nose over millions of lives."

"Uh . . . pick a nose, sir?" Dark Helmet asked.

"You know what I mean, Helmet," Skroob snarled. "Now, we'll forget your idiotic plan and do it my way. We'll use psychology."

"Psychology, sir?" Dark Helmet asked.

"Yes," Skroob said. "Send for the burning coals and the branding irons."

"Yes, sir." Colonel Sandurz, who had been watching everything from the far corner of the room, snapped to attention. "Karloff! Karloff!" he called.

"Yes, Master!" a voice boomed from the other room. In stepped Karloff, a huge monster of a man, wearing a traditional torturer's outfit, pushing a wagon that contained a bed of glowing red coals and several hot branding irons. "Hot stuff coming through. Watch your backs. Hot stuff!" he yelled.

"Very good, Karloff," Skroob said, smiling. His smile faded as he turned to Lord Helmet and said, "Helmet, take one of those branding irons and write *Skroob* all over her face."

"NO!" the Princess and the King screamed at once.

"Yes, Mr. President," Dark Helmet said. "And I thought *I* was mean!" he told himself. "I'm Strawberry Shortcake compared to him!"

Dark Helmet pulled on black asbestos gloves and reached for one of the branding irons. He began to pull one out, but Karloff reached a big hairy hand over and stopped him.

"I'd use a nine-iron, sir," Karloff said. "It's a soft lie."

"Thank you," Lord Helmet said, and pulled

a nine-iron from the fire. He gripped it tightly and approached the Princess.

"No, Daddy! No!" Vespa cried. "Don't tell them the combination — no matter what!"

But King Roland decided he had to give in. What if they were serious? Sure, no one had been serious for the first eighty pages or so of this book! But he couldn't take the chance. . . .

"Stop! Don't do anything!" the King shouted, a sweat of fear breaking out over his forehead. "I'll give you the combination."

"That's more like it," Skroob said. He pulled out a steno pad and a pencil. "Okay. The combination. Let's have it."

"Okay, okay," the King said, sounding defeated. "The combination is . . . one. . . ."

Skroob repeated it as he wrote it onto his pad. "One."

Dark Helmet also repeated it and wrote it down. "One."

"Two . . ." King Roland continued.

"Two," repeated Skroob.

"Two," said Dark Helmet, writing furiously.

"Three . . ." King Roland added.

"Three," Skroob repeated.

"Three," Dark Helmet said, writing it down.

"Four . . ." said King Roland.

"Four," repeated Skroob.

"Wait — not so fast!" cried Dark Helmet. "I'm getting behind here. What was the last number?"

"Four," Skroob told him.

Dark Helmet frantically erased what he had written down and put in a four.

"Five," King Roland said. "That's it. Now you have it." He lowered his head, feeling ashamed.

"Five?" Dark Helmet asked. "Do I have it right? It's one, two, three, four, five?"

"Yep. That's it," President Skroob replied. "I've got a more complicated combination on my gym locker!"

"I've told you what you want," the King interrupted. "Please release my daughter."

"We will. We will," Skroob told him. "Just as soon as we get our air."

Chapter 17

The evening mist fell silently on Spaceball City, draping the Ping-Pong ball buildings in a damp curtain of twilight. Two uniformed guards patrolled the wall at Prison Ball Twenty-eight, laser rifles on their shoulders.

Suddenly, the sky was filled with the roar of a descending spacecraft. The *Eagle Five* parted the thick mist as it came down for a hard landing in the prison yard, next to a sign that read: NO PARKING 12 A.M. TO 12 A.M. MONDAY THRU SUNDAY.

The two guards quickly pulled the rifles off their shoulders. "Hey! Can't you read? No parking!" one of them yelled up to the cockpit of the battered Winnebago.

They yanked open the door to Lone Starr's spaceship and ran inside, rifles at the ready. "Hands up!" the first guard yelled. "You're under arrest for illegal parking!"

Inside the ship, a loud scuffle ensued. A

few minutes later, two guards emerged from the ship and closed the door behind them. If anyone had looked closely, however, they would have noticed that one of the guards had a long, bushy tail!

Lone Starr and Barf, in their stolen Spaceball uniforms, made their way quickly into the Prison Ball. They hurried down a dark corridor until they came to a row of cells. A sign read: ROYAL PRISONERS ONLY. MAXIMUM SECURITY.

"Princess Vespa has got to be in one of these cells," Lone Starr said, pressing himself against the wall and motioning for Barf to follow him into the cell block.

Suddenly, they heard a booming, deep voice singing in one of the cells. "Nobody knows the trouble I've seen. . . ."

"That can't be her," Barf whispered.

Lone Starr slid open a panel in the door to the cell. ". . . Nobody knows but me . . ." sang the deep voice. They could see that it was Princess Vespa.

"Whaddaya know?" Lone Starr shrugged. "She sings bass!"

The Princess spun around, and her eyes grew wide. "Lone Starr — how did you find us?" She smiled, and they exchanged loving looks.

In the corner of the cell, Dot came out of Sleep Mode, and her mouth whirred open in surprise. "Lone Starr! Barf! Where did you — "

Lone Starr raised a finger to his lips. "Sshh. There's no time to talk. We've got to hightail it! Come on!"

He turned a laser key in the lock, and the cell door slid open. They began to run down the corridor.

"Stop!" Dot cried suddenly, lights flashing on her side. "I'm picking up electronic vibrations. Let me take a quick check."

She pressed her ABNORMAL VISION button, and her eyes began to glow with infrared light. "I thought so," she told them. "There's an invisible alarm beam ahead."

They followed her down the hall. "It's right here," she said. "Duck under. Be careful."

Dot ducked under the invisible beam, followed by Lone Starr, Vespa, and Barf. Barf ducked low enough, but he forgot about his tail. Sticking up behind him, it broke the invisible beam.

BLAAAAT. BLAAAAAT. A deafening alarm echoed down the corridor.

"Whoops. Sorry," Barf said, lowering his head. "You *said* to hightail it. I guess I didn't exactly get your meaning!"

"Never mind that now!" Lone Starr cried, as the alarm continued to blare. "Just run!"

They ran around the corner, and were greeted by a series of laser blasts. Four Spaceball guards, their laser rifles aglow, blocked the corridor. Our heroes stepped back. But more guards were coming from behind them.

"We're trapped!" Vespa cried.

"I've got an idea that might work," Barf said. He reached up to the wall and ripped off a bunch of curved Mylar tubes.

"Barf, what are you doing?" Lone Starr asked. "This is no time for arts and crafts!"

"Watch this," Barf said. He darted his head around the corner and stuck his tongue out at the guards. "Nyah-nah, nah-nyaah-nyaah!" he called.

The guards replied with a barrage of laser blasts. The clever mawg stuck out the Mylar tubes. The deadly laser beams zoomed into one end of the tubes and then shot out the other, right back at the guards. In seconds, the guards had blown themselves to bits!

"Hey — good plan!" Lone Starr cried, slapping Barf on the back.

But they didn't have long to celebrate. A squad of guards was right behind them. Our heroes ran over the four zapped guards and kept going down the corridor.

"Uh-oh!" Vespa cried.

Ahead of them, two huge, stainless steel slabs, one from the floor, one from the ceiling, began to close and seal off the corridor.

"Go for broke!" Lone Starr yelled. "Everybody dive on three! *Three*!!"

Side by side in unison, all four of them performed a spectacular, professional gymnastic tuck, roll, and dive.

CLAAAANG.

The slabs slammed together. But our

friends had just made it to the other side.

"We did it! We're home free!" Barf yelled.

But a voice in front of them told them he was mistaken. "Don't move or you're dead. We've got them, Captain!"

Chapter 18

The Spaceball Captain of the Guard, grinning in triumph, stepped up behind our four captured heroes.

"Sensational stunt, my friends," he said. "But it was a waste of time. Now clasp your hands behind your heads and slowly turn around."

The four prisoners clasped their hands behind their heads and slowly turned around. As they did so, the Captain's eyes bugged out of his head.

Standing before him were four men. Even the Princess was a man wearing a long, curly wig. He was badly in need of a shave, and smoking a short, black cigar.

"YOU IDIOTS!" the Captain exploded at his guards. "These are not them! You've captured their stunt doubles! Search the area! Find them! Find them!"

Having pulled the old stunt double switcheroo, Lone Starr and the others ran out of the Prison Ball and through the yard to the waiting *Eagle Five*. The alarm wailed loudly. Laser fire streamed through the air.

A laser blast hit the radio-TV antenna on top of the flying Winnebago. Another blast hit the door, fusing it to the side of the ship.

"We can't get in! The door is jammed!" Dot cried.

"Here. You hold them off," Lone Starr said. "Barf and I have to try to unjam the door."

Barf and Lone Starr tossed their rifles to Dot and the Princess. Vespa looked at the rifle in her hands and made a face. "Guns. Oooh, gross." She held it as if it were a smelly, dead fish. "I'm not shooting this. No way."

The troopers were advancing, firing their laser rifles. Dot took her rifle and began to shoot back. "No way," Vespa said, refusing to use her gun. "I don't believe in guns, you know. They're so . . . so violent."

Suddenly, a Spaceball laser ray came close, burning a tiny wisp of her hair. The Princess grabbed at the frizzed end, and her eyes grew wide in horror and disbelief. "My hair! Those creeps shot my *hair*!"

She dropped to one knee, raised and aimed the rifle, and in expert military fashion, fired off a series of quick rounds. One by one, the troopers dropped, mowed down by Vespa's deadly accurate barrage.

When the last trooper had been blown away, Vespa turned to Lone Starr. "Was that all right? Did I do okay?"

"Uh . . . sure. Not bad. . . ." Lone Starr had a little difficulty talking with his mouth hanging open in amazement.

He and Barf finally managed to pull the door open, and the four of them shoved into *Eagle Five,* closing the door behind them. A few seconds later, they lifted off, glad to leave Spaceball City behind.

Lone Starr and Barf sat in the cockpit, manning the controls with the Princess and Dot leaning over their shoulders. Lone Starr picked up the microphone and tried to make contact with Planet Druidia.

"King Roland, come in," he said. The telewall showed nothing but static. "This is *Eagle Five.* We have your daughter. We're heading for Planet Druidia."

Vespa grabbed the microphone away from him. "Daddy, I'm free. Change the combination to the air shield. Quick! The Spaceballs are on the way. Come in, Daddy. Come in. . . ."

"No good," Barf said, staring at the static-filled screen. "We can't get through. The televiewer is totally busted."

"Does this mean we can't watch *Wheel of Fortune?*" the worried Princess asked.

Chapter 19

As *Spaceball One* rumbled closer and closer to Planet Druidia, Dark Helmet, Sandurz, and President Skroob watched from the command center. Wide smiles crossed their faces as the planet's air shield came into view. Inside the shield could be seen fluffy white clouds, clear blue skies, and, beneath them, a lush green landscape.

"So, at last! Planet Druidia!" Skroob declared happily. "Ten thousand years of fresh air for our people to breathe!"

"Won't last us a hundred the way he runs things," Dark Helmet muttered under his breath.

"What?" Skroob asked.

"I said, Beautiful, isn't it," Dark Helmet replied.

"All right. Let's get on with it," Skroob ordered.

Sandurz snapped to attention. "Yes, Mr. President." He spoke into the intercom. "Prepare ship for metamorphosis."

"Ready, Kafka?" Lord Helmet called into the intercom.

"Ready, Lord Helmet," Kafka called back.

"Kafka? I thought his name was Chekhov," Skroob said, confused.

"You're thinking of another space show," Lord Helmet told him.

"How did a literary joke like that get into a book like this?" Skroob asked, totally confused.

As *Spaceball One* prepared its metamorphosis, the *Eagle Five* rumbled closer. "Look. It's *Spaceball One*," Lone Starr cried, pointing out the windscreen. "They've reached the air shield."

"Look — the air shield is opening!" the alarmed Dot cried.

"But their ship is too big," Lone Starr said. "Everyone knows it's the biggest, widest, longest ship ever built. They'll never get through."

"Yeah," Barf agreed. "How're they going to get the air out? I don't see hoses or anything."

"What — what's happening?" Vespa cried, staring out at Spaceball One. "Their ship — it's changing!"

"Omigosh!" Barf exclaimed, his ears shooting up in astonishment. "*Spaceball One* . . . it's not just a spaceship. It's a . . . Transformer!"

As our startled heroes watched, *Spaceball One* slowly transformed itself from a spaceship — into a gigantic robot MAID!

"Look — the maid has a vacuum cleaner!" Lone Starr exclaimed. "So *that's* how they're going to get the air!"

Spaceball One completely transformed into a robot maid holding a gigantic, upright vacuum cleaner. Its face and head, formerly the bridge area of the ship, vaguely resembled the face and head of the Statue of Liberty.

Inside the crown, Dark Helmet beamed proudly. "Metamorphosis completed," he announced. "*Spaceball One* has now become . . . Mega-Maid!"

"I DON'T DO WINDOWS!" came the booming voice of Mega-Maid.

"Commence Operation Vacu-Drive!" Dark Helmet commanded.

Instantly, the gigantic maid's hand reached down to the switch on the vacuum cleaner marked ON, OFF, and REVERSE. The robot thumb switched it to the ON position. Then Mega-Maid pushed the roaring vacuum cleaner to the open window of the air shield.

The fluffy white clouds were the first things to be sucked into the huge maw of the all-powerful vacuum cleaner. SWOOSH. An entire grove of trees were pulled straight up to the sky, and vanished, leaving only bare ground.

The vacuum cleaner moved over a snow-covered mountain. SWOOSH! The snowcap was sucked right off the mountaintop.

Mega-Maid moved the vacuum quickly, efficiently, sucking up all the air, all the atmosphere, everything in its path. . . .

In Castle Druidia, alone in his throne room, King Roland sat, holding a picture of his daughter, staring at it fondly, sadly. Gasping for air, he slumped back in his throne and closed his eyes. The Princess's picture fell to the floor with a clatter of breaking glass.

In a few seconds, there would be no air for the King or anyone else to breathe. Planet Druidia would be no more.

Chapter 20

Lone Starr and the others looked on helplessly from the cockpit of the *Eagle Five* as Mega-Maid continued to vacuum the atmosphere from Princess Vespa's beloved planet. "The air bag!" Vespa cried. "It's almost full. What'll we do?"

"I suppose they have a way to change the air bag," Barf said.

"That's *not* what I meant!" the Princess cried.

"We've got to act fast," Lone Starr said, staring straight ahead at the monstrous robot maid.

"Good thinking, Boss," Barf said, slapping him on the back.

Lone Starr ignored his sidekick's sarcasm. "Step One, we reverse that vacuum and blow the air back onto the planet. Step Two, we destroy that maid."

"But isn't that dangerous?" Vespa asked, her voice filled with concern.

"Extremely," Lone Starr told her, taking

her hand. "Plus, I don't know how the heck we're gonna do it!"

They stared at each other in silence. Mega-Maid's vacuum cleaner continued to roar.

"How about that ring Yogurt gave you?" Barf suggested.

"Oh, yeah." Lone Starr snapped his fingers. "I forgot about it. Now, where'd I put that thing? I think I lost it." He began to search his pockets.

Barf groaned and threw up his hands. "You lose everything," he told Lone Starr. "Your library card, your bus pass, and now . . . the Ring of the Schwartz."

"Is this what you're looking for?" Vespa asked. She picked the silver ring up from the control panel.

"Yeah. That's it," Lone Starr said, taking it from her and slipping it onto his middle finger. "Okay. Here goes nothing."

He stepped up to the windscreen and pointed his finger at the switch on the vacuum cleaner. Then he concentrated with all his might. The others watched in suspense as the ring began to glow and then hum.

"It . . . it's working!" Barf cried.

The force of the Schwartz slowly turned the vacuum's switch from ON to OFF. The deafening roar of the vacuum immediately ceased.

"Come on, Schwartz! Come on, Schwartz!" Barf cried, jumping up and down like a cheerleader.

With a resounding click that echoed off

the stars, the vacuum switched from OFF to REVERSE. The vacuum roared to life again, this time blowing the air back into the planet. The air bag quickly deflated.

Down in King Roland's throne room, the drapes began to blow. Vespa's photograph began to flutter on the floor. The King took a deep breath of fresh air and opened his eyes. "Hey! I'm breathing! I'm breathing air!" he cried. He jumped up jubilantly. "Air! I love it! I love air!"

Outside the castle, the grove of trees plopped back down in place. The snowcap dropped back onto the mountaintop. The clouds popped one by one back into the sky. The people of Druidia took a deep breath and began to celebrate.

But up on the *Eagle Five*, there was no time for celebration. "Let's go," Lone Starr said grimly. "We've got to destroy the maid now."

"Couldn't we just give her two weeks' notice?" the Princess asked.

Lone Starr was concentrating too hard to hear her. He guided the *Eagle Five* into the dark hole of Mega-Maid's ear. The windscreen went black as they flew inside the immense robot's head.

Lone Starr flicked on the scanner and studied it as he guided the spaceship. "There's got to be a self-destruct mechanism somewhere in the central brain area," he said, staring into the screen.

The scanner began to beep. "I think I

found it," Lone Starr told them. "There it is, right below us in the ear canal. Put her in hover, Barf. I'm going down there."

A few moments later, the courageous Lone Starr was descending the rope ladder from the *Eagle Five*. He dropped to the floor of the ear canal. He looked around, opened a door marked: EMERGENCY EXIT, and went in. He didn't realize that he had tripped a silent alarm.

High above in the bridge area, Dark Helmet and the other Spaceballs were in a state of confusion. "What's going on? What happened to Mega-Maid?" Dark Helmet cried. "Why is it so hard to get good help these days?"

Suddenly, the radar operator interrupted. "Sir, I'm picking up a silent alarm in the self-destruct complex."

Dark Helmet hurried over to the security monitor. On the screen, he saw a familiar figure making his way down one of the lower corridors.

"Lone Starr!" Dark Helmet cried.

"I'll call the guards," Sandurz said.

"No!" Dark Helmet held him back. "He's mine!" He slipped on his onyx ring. "I'll handle this. . . ."

Down in the self-destruct center, Lone Starr crept up on a door that said: NO UNAUTHORIZED OR AUTHORIZED PERSONNEL PERMITTED TO ENTER. He overpowered the guard with a quick karate chop and quickly entered the inner ear chamber.

Focusing his eyes in the darkness, he saw the self-destruct mechanism at one end. On the other end was the guard's quarters, a stainless steel bunk bed, a locker, and a small washstand.

A guard stood shaving at the sink, his face covered with shaving cream. A large towel on a rack beside him had a huge picture of Dark Helmet on it, and the words: SPACEBALLS — THE TOWEL.

Startled at seeing another guard, Lone Starr reached for his gun. He didn't have it.

"Is that you, Mylar?" the guard called over his shoulder.

Lone Starr looked desperately for a weapon. He spotted something. A can of shaving cream stood on the washstand. The label read: SPACEBALLS — THE SHAVING CREAM.

Lone Starr aimed the Ring of the Schwartz at the shaving cream and concentrated with all his might. The shaving cream can began to tremble. Then it floated right into Lone Starr's waiting hand.

The guard spun around. "What the — Who are you?" he cried.

"You forgot your eyes," Lone Starr said. SPLURT SPLURT. With two quick bursts, he covered the guard's eyes with shaving cream. The guard opened his mouth to scream for help. But Lone Starr filled that with shaving cream, too. Then a quick karate chop dropped the helpless guard.

Lone Starr hurried over to the self-destruct mechanism. He found it inside a Lucite case. Below it, a sign read: SELF-DESTRUCT BUTTON: DO NOT PUSH UNLESS YOU REALLY REALLY MEAN IT.

Lone Starr really *really* meant it. He raised his finger and prepared to push the self-destruct button.

But he was interrupted by a voice from behind him. "Not so fast . . ." Dark Helmet said.

Chapter 21

Lone Starr whirled around to face his opponent. "Dark Helmet!" he cried.

"So, Lone Starr," said Dark Helmet, his voice sounding tinny and distant behind his visor, "at last we meet for the first time for the last time."

"Wha?" Lone Starr asked.

Dark Helmet flipped up his visor. "I said, So, Lone Starr, at last we meet for the first time for the last time."

"Oh," Lone Starr replied.

There wasn't time for any more of this sparkling conversation. Dark Helmet raised his ring and pointed it at Lone Starr. A force beam shot off the ring.

Lone Starr raised his ring just in time, and blocked the shot with his own beam. The room crackled with an explosion of flaring energy.

"What the — How d'ja do that?" Dark Helmet cried in surprise. "If there's anything I despise, it's a fair fight," he scowled. "But if

I must, I must. May the best man win." He extended his hand.

Lone Starr reached forward and shook hands with him. And when he pulled back his hand, the ring was no longer on his finger. Dark Helmet had palmed it.

"Ha-ha! You fool!" Dark Helmet tossed the ring to the floor. They both watched it roll down a grate. "Now, say good-bye," sneered Dark Helmet.

Lone Starr took a step back, but there was nowhere to run. The deadly green beam shot out of Dark Helmet's ring. Lone Starr took a deep breath and executed a spectacular, Baryshnikov-type ballet leap and midair split, touching his toes with his hands.

"Bravo! Bravo!" Dark Helmet cheered. "But what do you do for an encore?"

Dark Helmet moved closer, raising the ring for another shot. Lone Starr shielded himself with his hands. He realized he was trapped and helpless.

Suddenly, he heard the voice of Yogurt, echoing in his mind. "Use the Schwartz, Lone Starr. Use the Schwartz."

"I can't. I lost the ring," Lone Starr said.

"I know you did," Dark Helmet told him, looking around to see who he was talking to. "I was there, remember?"

"Forget the ring. The ring is *bupkis*," the voice of Yogurt told Lone Starr. "I found it in a Crackerjack box. It was never the ring. It was you. It was always you."

Lone Starr's face filled with confusion. He

couldn't decide whether to believe Yogurt or not. But, he realized, what choice did he have? One direct hit from Dark Helmet's ring, and he'd be yogurt himself!

Out of the corner of his eye, Lone Starr spotted the shaving mirror on the shelf above the sink. He closed his eyes and concentrated.

A triumphant grin spread across Dark Helmet's face. "Here it comes, Lone Starr," he said, aiming his ring.

The mirror flew into Lone Starr's hand. The beam shot out of Dark Helmet's ring — reflected off the mirror — and slammed back into Dark Helmet with helmet-shattering force.

"Noooooo! Hoo, boy!" Dark Helmet screamed and crumpled to the floor, writhing in agony.

Lone Starr put down the mirror. "Maybe that'll give you something to reflect on, Dark Helmet," he said. Then he ran to the Lucite case, flipped the lid open, and determinedly pressed the self-destruct button.

Alarms rang out. Sirens wailed. The screams of terrified crew members filled the vast chambers of Mega-Maid.

Up top, Colonel Sandurz picked up the intercom mike and began screaming. "Attention. Attention. Abandon spaceship. Abandon spaceship. Why am I repeating everything? Why am I repeating everything? Let's just get out of here! All personnel proceed to escape pods."

His frantic announcement set off a wild stampede as all the crew members leaped up from their posts and ran to the escape pods.

A few seconds later, everyone had left. "In exactly thirty seconds," the mechanical voice on the loudspeaker announced, "this ship will self-destruct."

Suddenly, Sandurz and Dark Helmet appeared back on the bridge. "Somebody stole my pod," Sandurz said, looking dazed.

"Somebody stole *my* pod," Dark Helmet said, sounding equally surprised.

"Nobody stole my pod!" President Skroob announced from across the chamber. He opened the door and started in. "So long, boys. It's been great."

"Oh, no, you don't!" Sandurz pulled Skroob out of the escape pod. Immediately, Dark Helmet leaped in and started to buckle himself up.

"Oh, no, you don't!" President Skroob grabbed Dark Helmet and pulled him out. While they wrestled, Sandurz climbed in.

"Oh, no, you don't!" Dark Helmet grabbed Sandurz and pulled him out. Skroob jumped back in and pulled the lever. Dark Helmet and Sandurz pulled him out.

The doors closed.

The pod took off.

The three Spaceballs stood and stared at each other. "You idiot!" they cried in unison.

"In exactly ten seconds," announced the loudspeaker, "this ship will self-destruct.

Counting down. Ten, nine, eight, six — "

"Wait! What happened to seven?" Skroob cried.

"Just kidding!" said the loudspeaker. "Seven, five, four. . . ."

Skroob, Dark Helmet, and Sandurz huddled together in the bridge, clutching each other desperately.

". . . Three, two, one. . . . Zero. Have a nice day."

A blinding orange-white light was followed by an explosion that rocked the galaxy. The head and arm of Mega-Maid sailed off into the heavens as the rest of the gigantic craft broke into tiny bits that flew in every direction.

Seconds before the explosion to end all explosions, the *Eagle Five* had burst out of Mega-Maid's ear, roaring away at full throttle.

"Yahoo! We made it!" Barf cried.

Then they watched the awesome explosion as the Spaceball craft self-destructed and knew that victory really was theirs.

"You did it!" Princess Vespa cried happily to Lone Starr. "I don't know how — but you did it!"

"Nothin' to it," Lone Starr said nonchalantly. "In one ear and out the other."

And then he fainted.

Chapter 22

Carrying its four happy passengers, the *Eagle Five* flew through the opening in the air shield and into the beautiful skies of Planet Druidia. As Lone Starr guided the ship down, Barf took a quick snooze, his big feet up on the control panel. Suddenly, his foot slipped. He kicked the intercom switch. Lone Starr found himself eavesdropping on the Princess in the rear compartment.

"I don't care," Vespa was saying to Dot, her voice filled with emotion. "I don't love Prince Valium. I love Lone Starr."

"You have no choice, my dear," Dot's voice came over the intercom. "You are a princess. You must marry a prince."

"I don't care," Vespa whined. "I love Lone Starr, and I know he loves me. I can see it in his eyes. I'd give up everything for him. Everything. And I'm going to tell him right now."

Lone Starr's face filled with surprise. Thinking quickly, he realized that, despite his feelings for her, he couldn't let the Princess throw away everything for him.

He shook Barf awake. "Listen," he whispered, "whatever I say, just go along with it — understand?"

"Huh? Wha?" Barf was still half asleep.

In his rearview mirror, Lone Starr saw the Princess entering the cockpit. He began talking loudly to Barf, pretending to be in the middle of a conversation. "In love with the Princess? Are you kidding? It was all an act."

The Princess stopped at the curtain, hurt and bewildered.

"But you told me you thought she was terrific," Barf replied, not catching on.

Lone Starr gave him a hard kick under the control panel and pointed back to the curtain. "Yeah, a terrifically silly, self-centered, spoiled brat," Lone Starr said.

"Oh, yeah. Yeah. That was it," Barf said, finally getting it.

"I can't wait to get rid of her and collect that reward — a million spacebucks," Lone Starr continued loudly.

Tears began to roll down Vespa's cheek. She turned and ran back to the rear compartment.

"I don't know what you had in mind," Barf said to Lone Starr, shaking his head. "But if you wanted her to stop loving you, you sure did a good job."

Lone Starr frowned and looked away. "Yeah, well, I wasn't gonna let her give up being a princess just so she can hang out with a space bum for the rest of her life."

Barf shrugged. "Have it your way. I think I'll watch some TV."

He turned on the TV set. A computerized newsman appeared on the screen. "And on a sadder note," the newsman said, "Pizza the Hutt, half man, half pizza, was found dead earlier this morning in his Vega condominium. Cause of death was reported to be suicide. He got locked in his room and ate himself to death. Coming up next, Gary's review of *Rocky Ten Thousand. . . .*"

Barf clicked off the TV. "Hey, Boss, didja hear that?" he asked. "Pizza kicked the bucket. Now we don't have to pay him the million. We can keep it all."

"Yeah," Lone Starr said glumly. "I heard."

He wasn't thinking about the million space-bucks he'd get to keep. He was thinking about the beautiful Princess he'd just lost.

Chapter 23

Happiness and celebration reigned on Planet Druidia. The planet's atmosphere had been returned. Their beautiful Princess had been rescued and brought home. And her wedding to Prince Valium was about to be held again.

In the First Intergalactic Temple, Vespa, back in her wedding gown, stood at the top of the aisle, ready to walk down to her sleepy-eyed groom. "Are you all right, my dear?" King Roland asked. "You *will* stop when you reach the altar this time, won't you?"

"Don't worry, Father," Vespa said. "I'm completely over that pilot. He didn't even stay for the wedding. Just grabbed his million spacebucks and ran."

"But he didn't take the million," King Roland told her.

Vespa gasped in surprise. "He didn't?"

"No," the King said. "He just took two hundred and forty-eight spacebucks for lunch, gas, and tolls."

"The Wedding March" began. King Roland offered Vespa his hand, and they started down the aisle. Prince Valium yawned up at her as she approached, but the Princess didn't see him. Her mind was spinning from what her father had just told her.

Thousands of miles away in space, Lone Starr glumly guided the *Eagle Five.* "I still can't believe you turned down the money!" Barf cried for the eight-thousandth time. "At least we could've stayed for the wedding feast. I'm starving! We got anything to eat?"

"No," Lone Starr said, lost in melancholy thoughts. "Oh. Wait a minute." He reached into his shirt pocket. "Yogurt gave me a fortune cookie. You can have it."

Barf eagerly took the cookie and broke it open. But instead of a paper fortune, a shimmering ray of light poured out of the cookie. The light quickly formed itself into the figure of Yogurt.

"Hiya, fellas. How's it goin'? Nice to see ya. How ya been?" the image of Yogurt said cheerfully. "Ready for your fortune? You know that medallion you wear around your neck that you don't know what it means?"

"Yes," Lone Starr said.

"Don't interrupt a holographic recording," Yogurt scolded. "Well . . . it's a royal birth certificate. Your father was a king. Your mother was a queen. Which makes you a certified prince."

"Hey! I'm a prince! Whaddaya know!" Lone Starr's mood changed immediately. "That means. . . ."

"That means, if you hurry, there could be a princess in your future," Yogurt said. "Now, if you want to get back there before she marries Sleeping Beauty, there's a can of special fuel in your glove compartment." With a shimmer of light, the image of Yogurt faded and disappeared.

"Barf! Quick! Open the glove compartment!" Lone Starr cried.

Barf pulled open the glove compartment and pulled out a small can. It was labeled LIQUID SCHWARTZ.

"Wow! Liquid Schwartz! What's the octane on that?" Barf exclaimed.

"Just pour it in the gas tank!" Lone Starr said impatiently. "Then, hang on, Barf-O — we're gonna make spacetracks!"

A few seconds later, the sound of screeching rubber echoed through space as the *Eagle Five* made a sharp U-turn. Then the ship sped off so fast it left skid marks in the sky.

Chapter 24

"Dearly beloved," began the minister, standing before the royal couple. "We are gathered here together . . . again . . . to join — "

"Why didn't you tell me he didn't take the money?" Vespa asked her father, who was standing behind her.

"I didn't think it was important," King Roland whispered.

"May we continue, please?" the annoyed minister asked. "We are gathered here to join Princess Vespa and Prince — "

"I see it all now," the Princess said loudly to her father. "He said all those terrible things so I'd hate him. He was sacrificing himself so I wouldn't give up the throne. Don't you see? He loves me!"

"Excuse me," the minister broke in. "I'm trying to conduct a wedding here, which has nothing to do with love. Knock it off, okay, Your Highness?"

"I'm sorry," Vespa said.

The minister began again. But this time he was interrupted by the roar of *Eagle Five*'s engines as it landed outside the temple. "That's him! I know it's him! He's come back!" Vespa cried.

"That's it!" the exasperated minister cried. "I'm not taking any more chances. We're doing the short version." He began speaking as fast as he could. "Do-you-Prince-Valium-take-Princess-Vespa-to-be-yourlaw-fullyweddedwife?

"I do," Valium said dreamily.

"Princess - Vespa - do - you - take - Prince - Valium - to - beyourlawfullyweddedhusband?" the minister asked.

"She *doesn't*!" called a voice from the rear of the temple.

All eyes turned to see Lone Starr, resplendent in a white-and-gold-silk prince outfit — and even clean-shaven! Beside him, Barf looked as if he had just had a fancy grooming at a Beverly Hills poodle parlor.

"Who are you?" the minister called out.

"Prince Lone Starr!" the shiny new Lone Starr declared proudly.

"You're a prince?" Vespa cried.

"Yeah. Do you believe it? I just found out," Lone Starr told her, pointing to his medallion. "I'm an honest-to-goodness certified prince. Will you marry me?"

"Wait," the Princess replied. "Let me think it over. *YES*!"

"I'm sick of this," the minister said, stamping his foot. "I don't care who it is, but I'm going to marry *somebody* today." He pointed to Lone Starr. "You! Get down here!"

A wide grin spread across Lone Starr's face as he ambled down the aisle. Barf rushed ahead, picked up Prince Valium as if he were a potted plant, and set him down in a pew. "Excuse me. We won't be needing you anymore," Barf said to him.

"Oh. All right." Valium yawned.

"Okay, here we go," the minister said as Lone Starr stepped to the Princess's side. "The short short version." He looked at Lone Starr. "Do you?"

"Yes," Lone Starr said.

The minister looked at Vespa. "Do you?"

"Yes," Vespa said.

"You're married. Kiss the bride."

As Lone Starr and Vespa kissed, all of the bells on Planet Druidia began to chime out in celebration. Seeing them together, everyone in the temple knew that they would live happily ever after — or until *Spaceballs Two* — whichever came first!

Millions of miles away in another galaxy, a beautiful blue marble of a planet, a planet of green earth and gently rolling seas, spun silently on its orbit around a warming sun.

Suddenly, two objects fell from the sky and landed on the planet with a resounding *plop*. The first object was Mega-Maid's huge head, which landed upright in the sand. Beside it, landed her right arm, still holding the vacuum handle, which pointed skyward. The strange structures looked surprisingly like the top of the Statue of Liberty.

After a few moments, three small figures began to lower themselves one by one from her left nostril. Clinging to a knotted rope of bedsheets were Dark Helmet, Sandurz, and Skroob.

In the distance, two riders, seeing this strange sight, reigned in their horses. The riders were apes, wearing dark robes.

"What are those things coming out of her nose?" the first ape asked, shielding his eyes with his hand.

The second ape looked through a pair of binoculars. "Spaceballs!" he exclaimed.

"Uh-oh," declared the first ape. "There goes the planet!"

THE END